FOR ORGANS, PIANOS & ELECTRONIC KEYBOARDS

93

2nd Edition

Country Hits

G000078452

Contents

ISBN-13: 978-0-7935-1673-5
ISBN-10: 0-7935-1673-0

7777 W. BLUEMOUND RD. P.O. BOX 13819 MILWAUKEE, WI 53213

E-Z Play ® TODAY Music Notation © By 1975 HAL LEONARD CORPORATION

E-Z PLAY and EASY ELECTRONIC KEYBOARD MUSIC are registered trademarks of HAL LEONARD CORPORATION.

Visit Hal Leonard Online at
www.halleonard.com

All the Gold in California

Registration 3
Rhythm: Swing

Words and Music by
Larry Gatlin

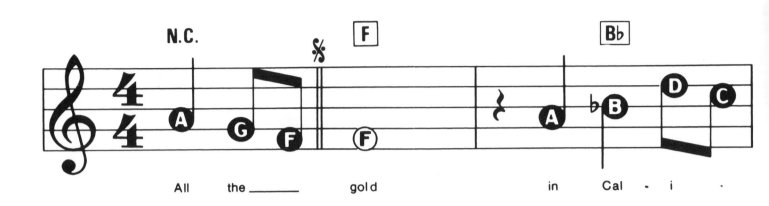

All the _____ gold in Cal - i -

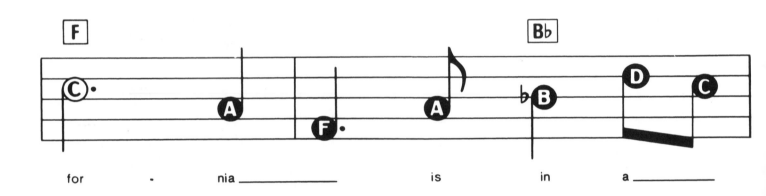

for - nia _____ is in a _____

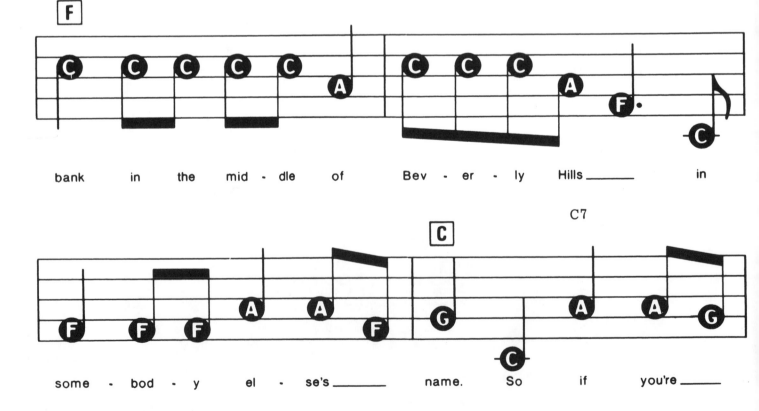

bank in the mid - dle of Bev - er - ly Hills _____ in

some - bod - y el - se's _____ name. So if you're _____

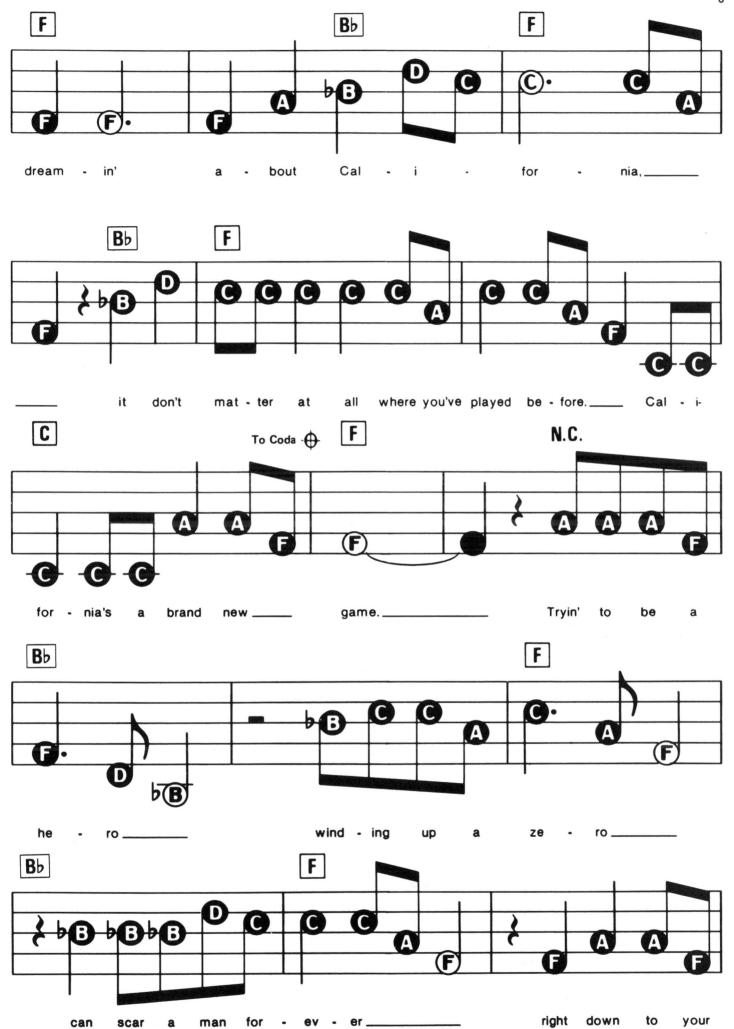

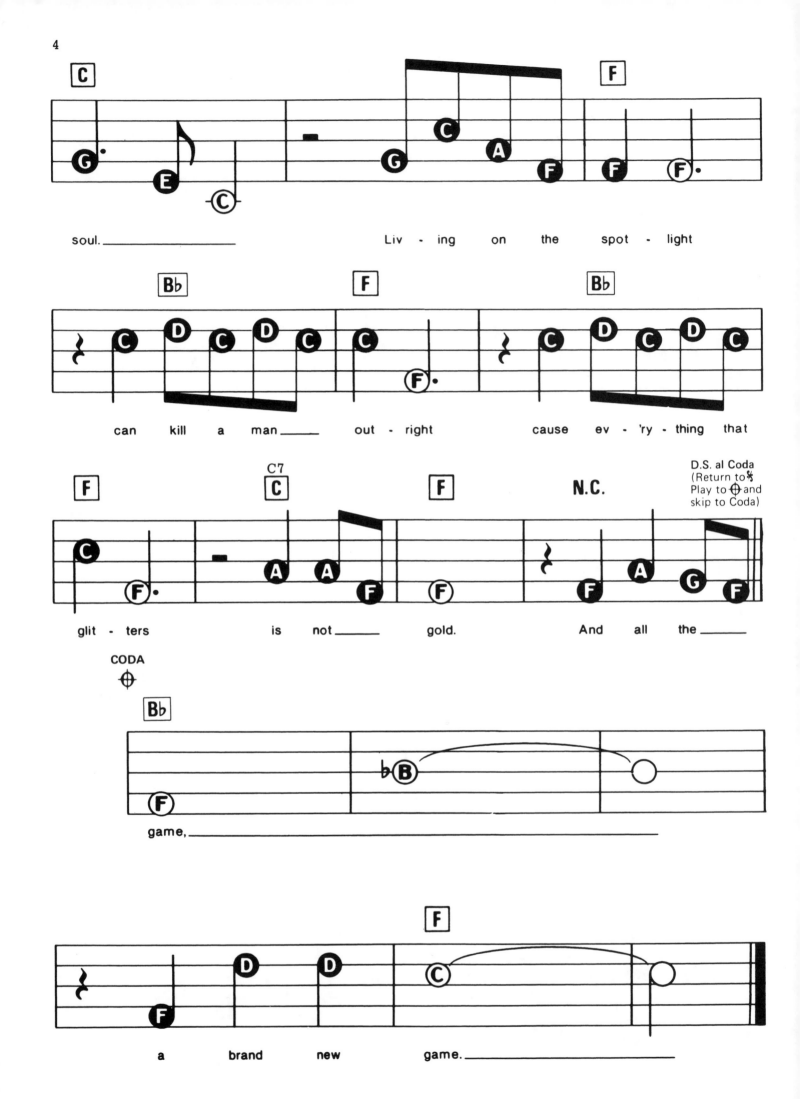

soul._____ Liv - ing on the spot - light

can kill a man____ out - right cause ev - 'ry - thing that

glit - ters is not____ gold. And all the____

game,_____

a brand new game._____

By the Time I Get to Phoenix

Registration 8
Rhythm: 8 Beat or Rock

Words and Music by
Jimmy Webb

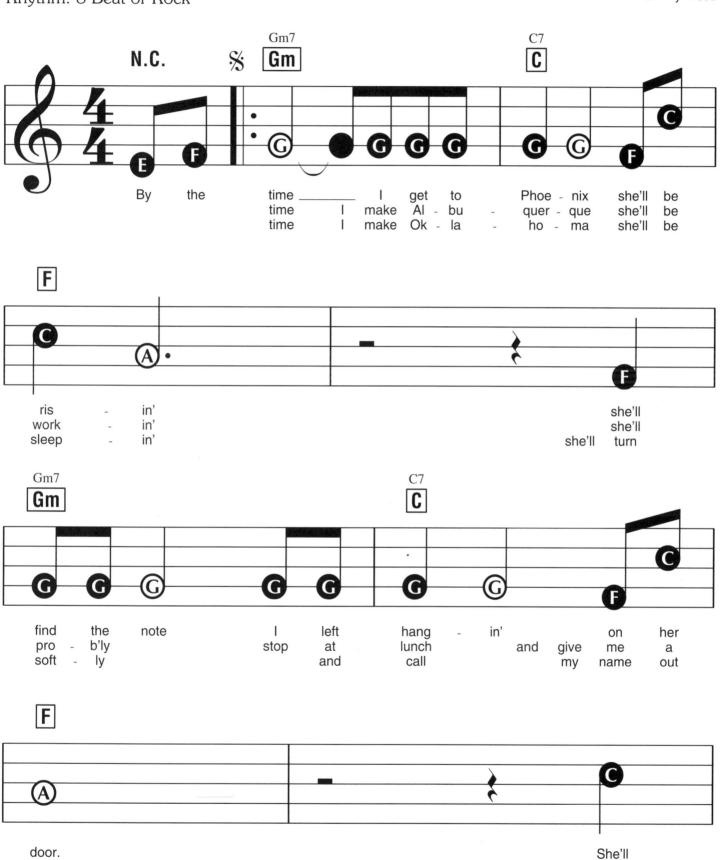

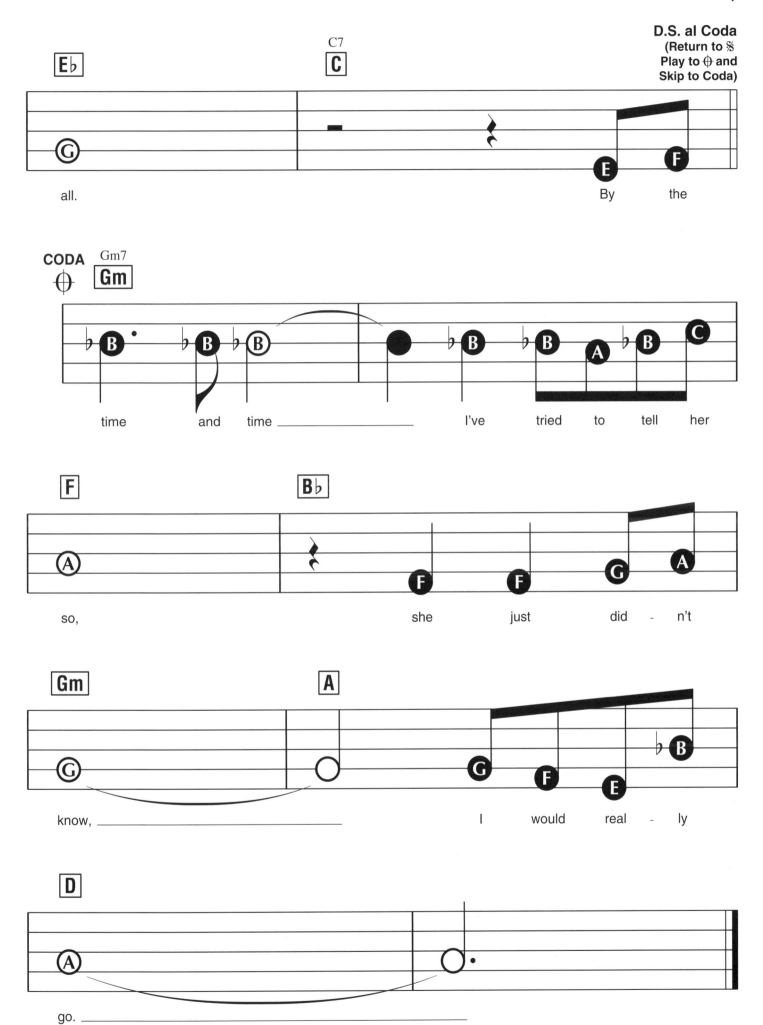

Baby I Lied

Registration 9
Rhythm: Rock

Words and Music by Rafe VanHoy,
Rory Michael Bourke and Deborah Allen

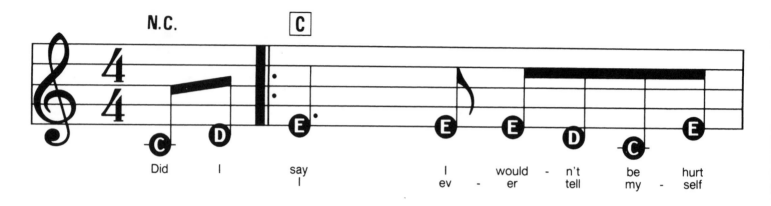

Did I say I would - n't be hurt
ev - er tell my - self

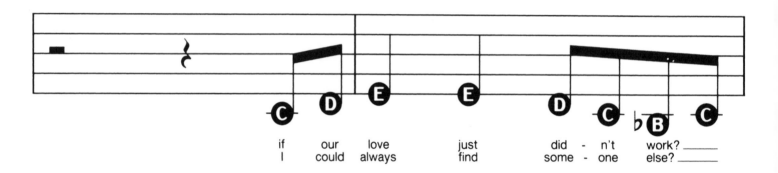

if our love just did - n't work?
I could always find some - one else?

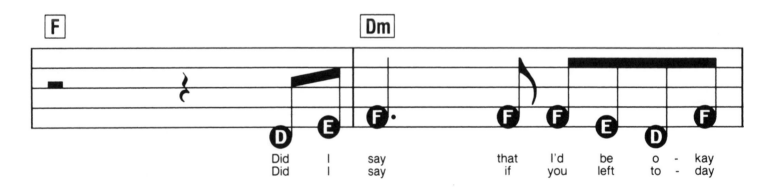

Did I say that I'd be o - kay
Did I say if you left to - day

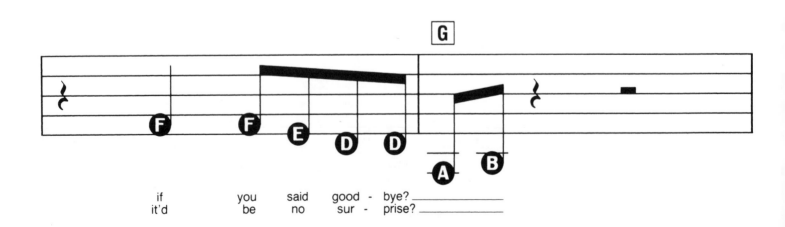

if you said good - bye?
it'd be no sur - prise?

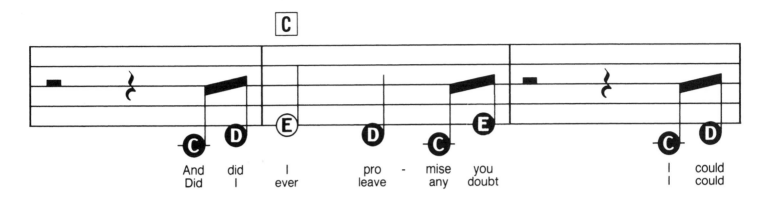

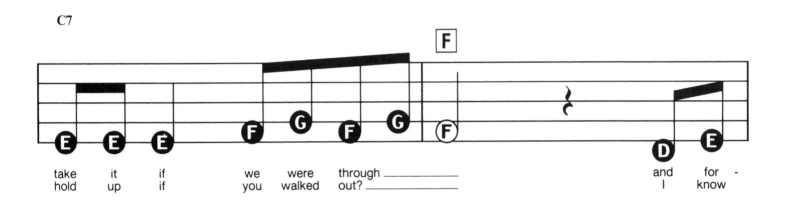

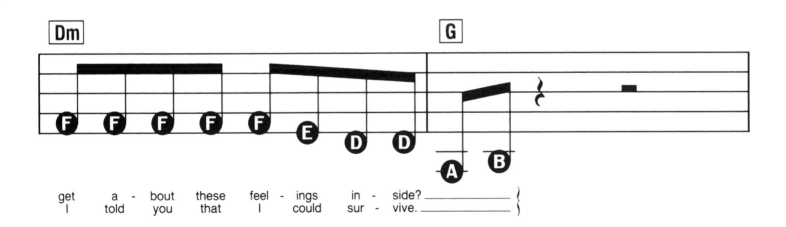

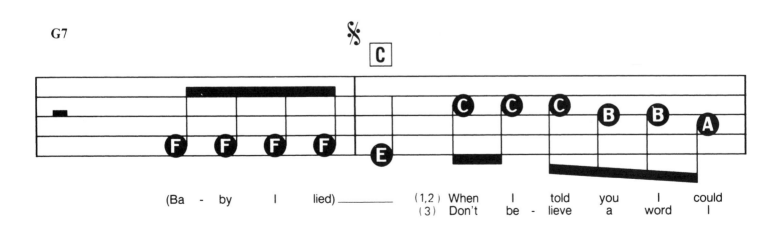

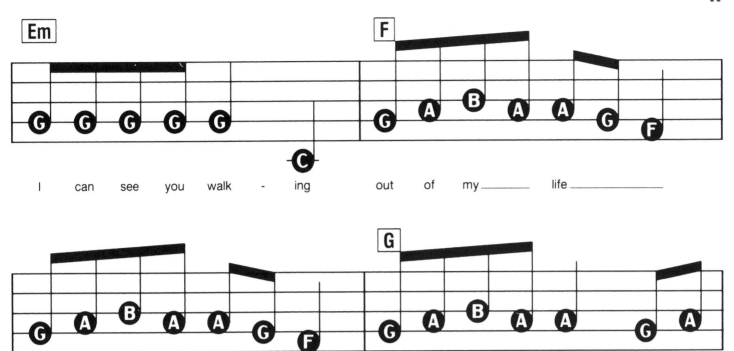

I can see you walk - ing out of my ____ life ____

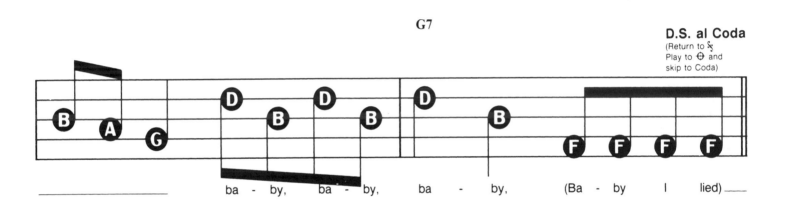

say - ing good - bye, ____ I re - al - ize, ____

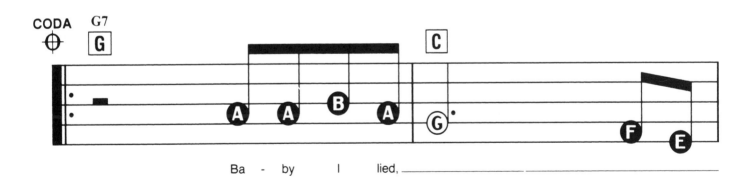

____ ba - by, ba - by, ba - by, (Ba - by I lied) ____

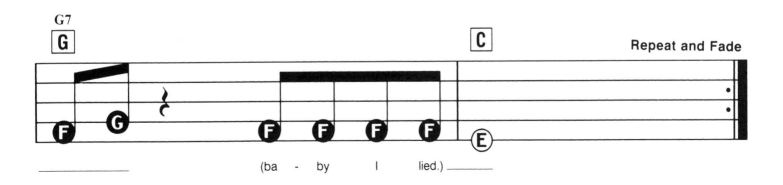

Ba - by I lied, ____

(ba - by I lied.) ____

The Closer You Get

Registration 4
Rhythm: Country or Shuffle

Words and Music by James Pennington
and Mark Gray

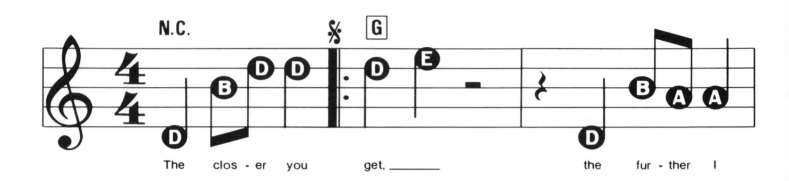

The clos-er you get, _____ the fur-ther I

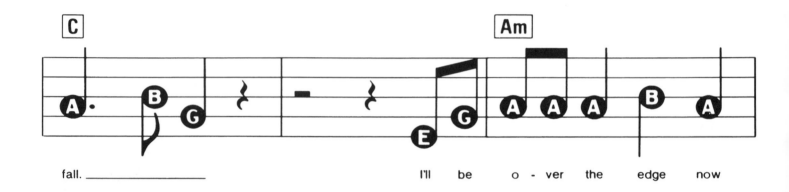

fall. _____ I'll be o-ver the edge now

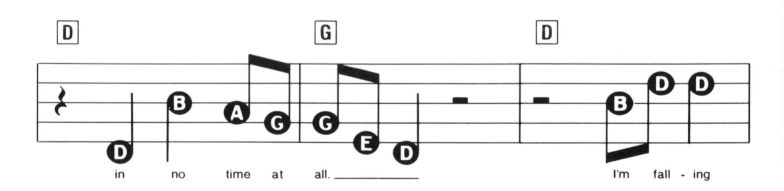

in no time at all. _____ I'm fall-ing

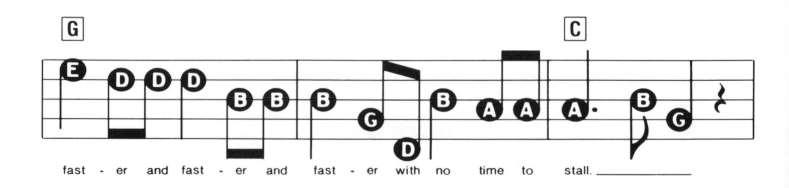

fast-er and fast-er and fast-er with no time to stall. _____

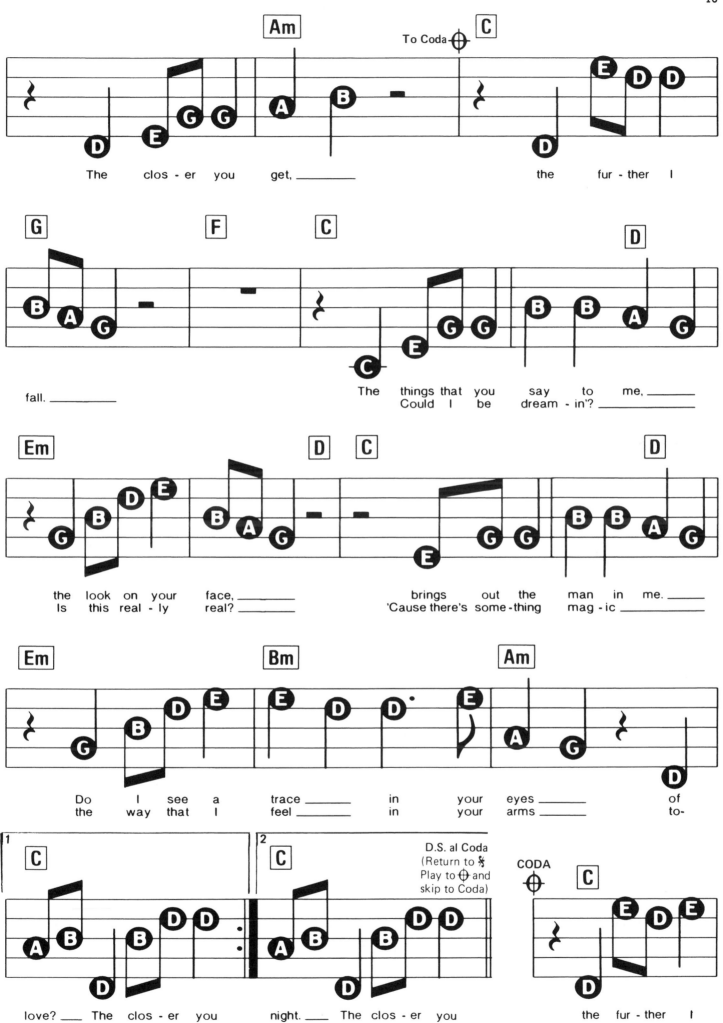

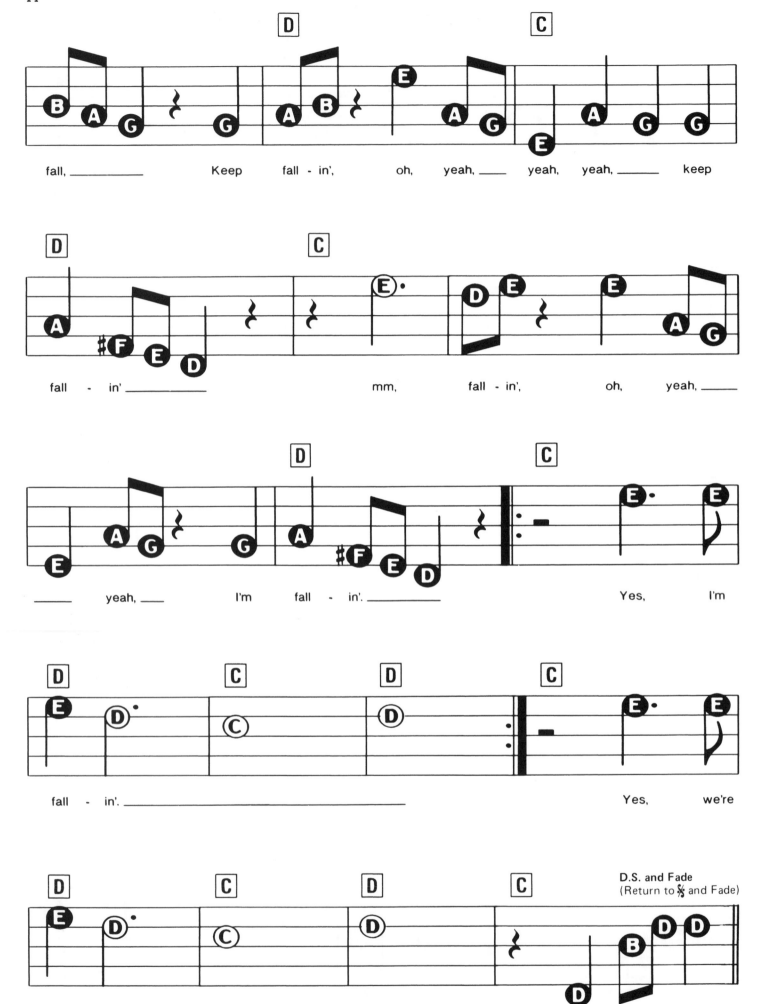

Daytime Friends

Registration 2
Rhythm: Country or Swing

Words and Music by
Ben Peters

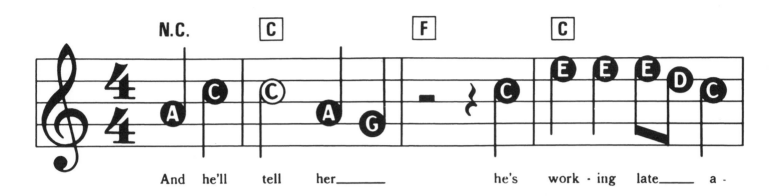

And he'll tell her_____ he's work-ing late_____ a-

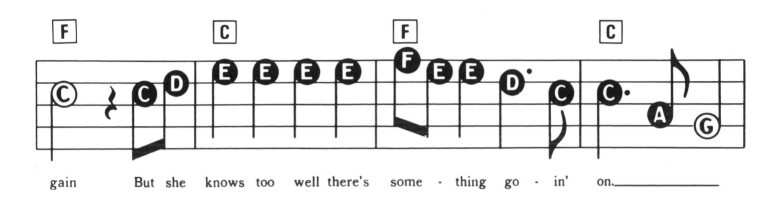

gain But she knows too well there's some - thing go - in' on._____

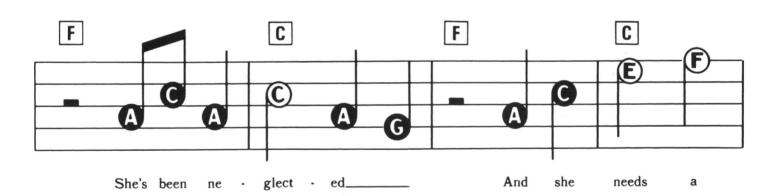

She's been ne - glect - ed_____ And she needs a

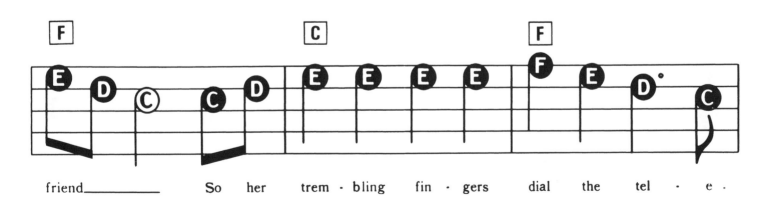

friend_____ So her trem - bling fin - gers dial the tel - e -

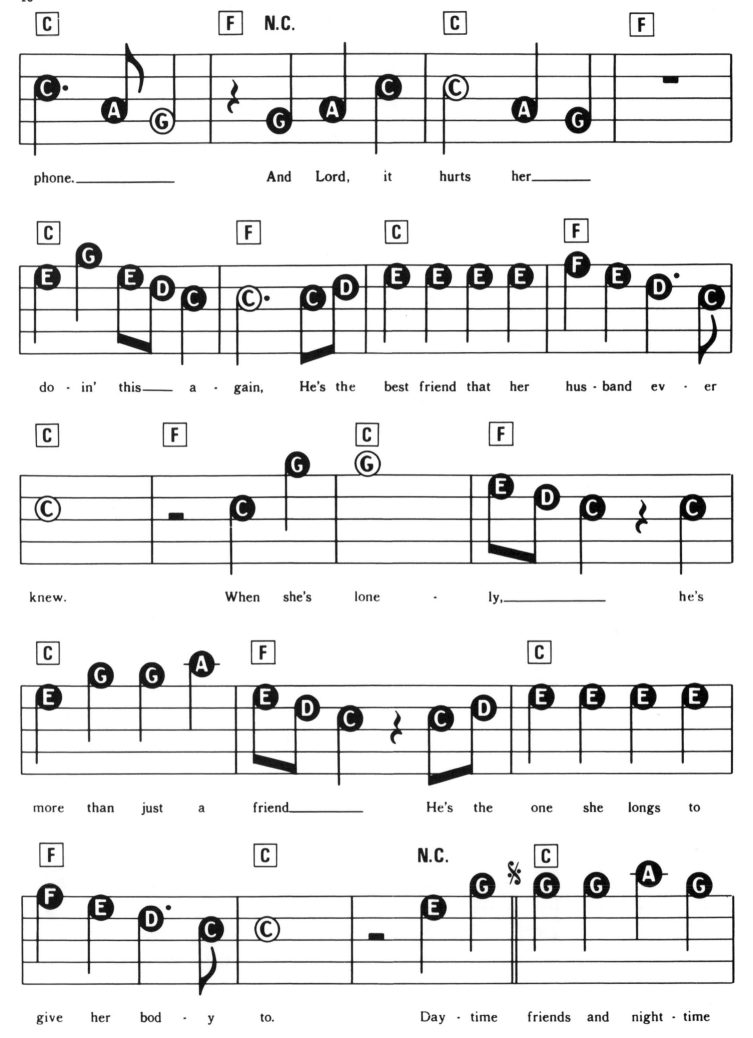

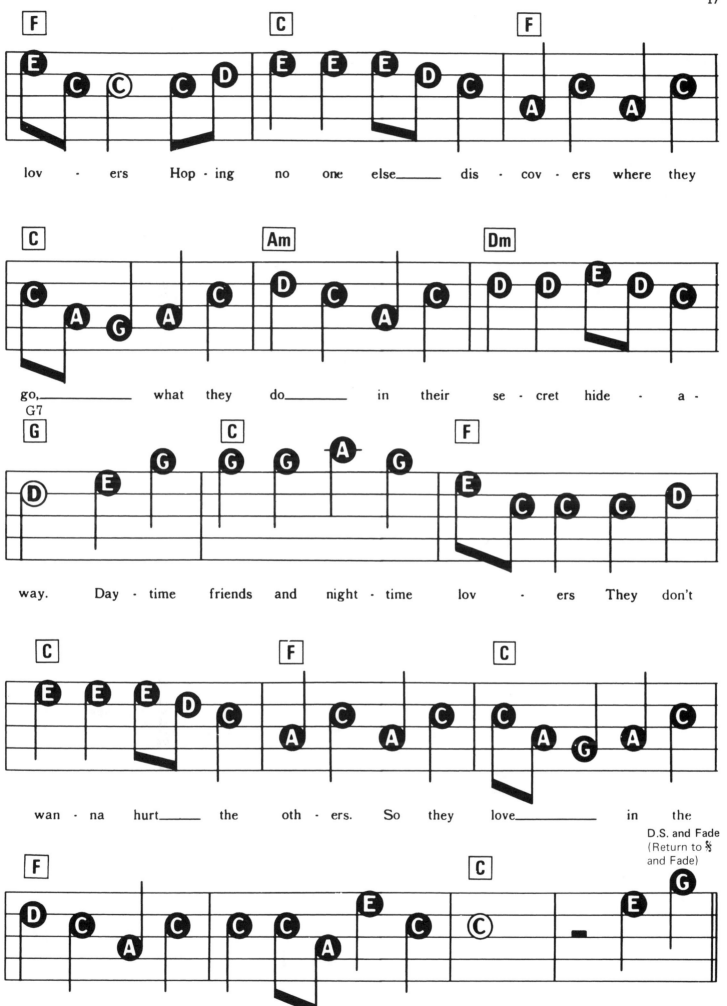

Coward of the County

Registration 7
Rhythm: Country Western

Words and Music by Roger Bowling
and Billy Edd Wheeler

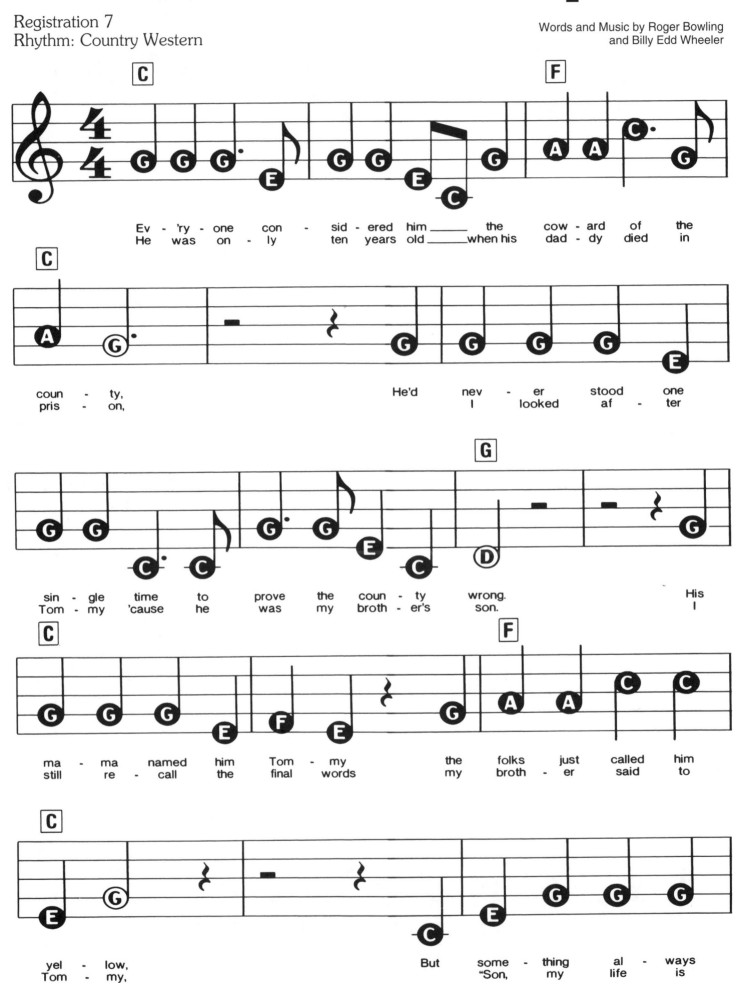

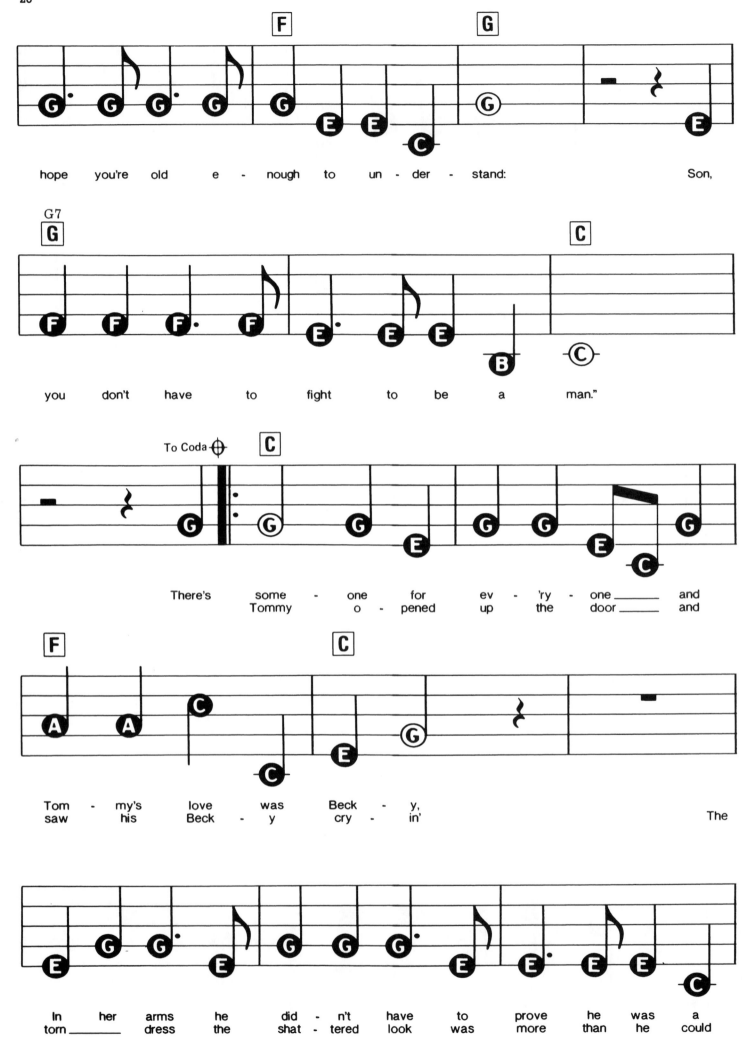

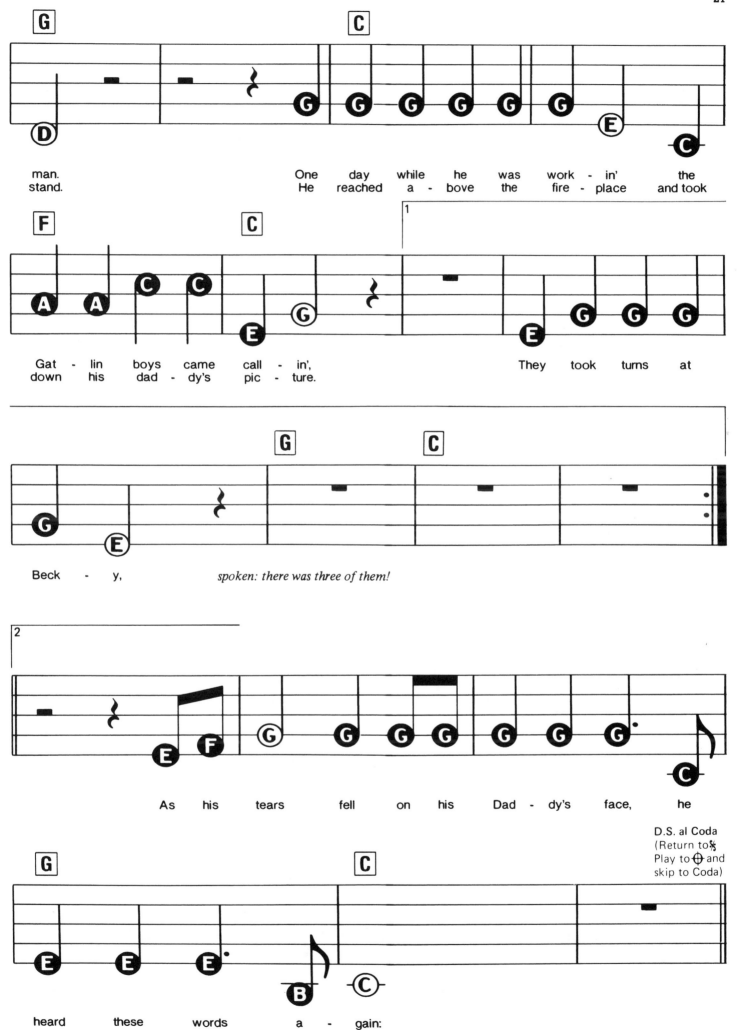

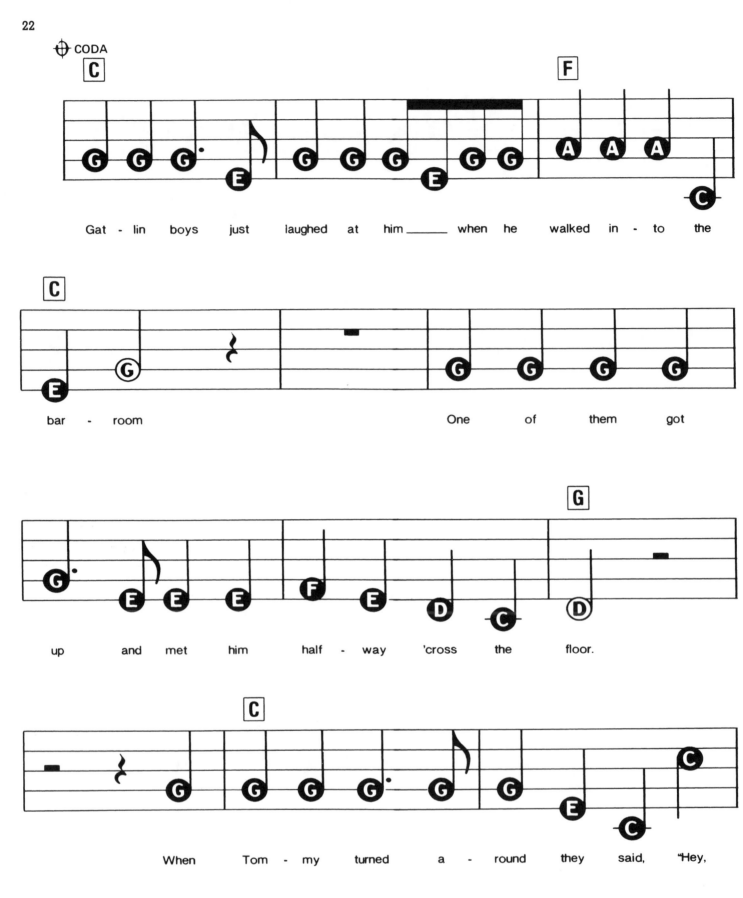

Gat - lin boys just laughed at him _____ when he walked in - to the bar - room   One of them got up and met him half - way 'cross the floor.   When Tom - my turned a - round they said, "Hey,

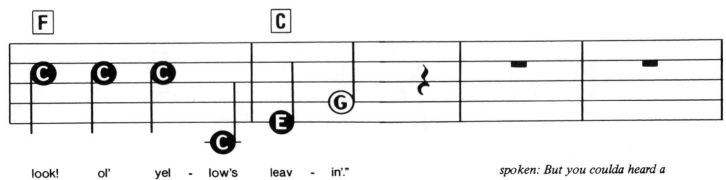

look! ol' yel - low's leav - in'."   *spoken: But you coulda heard a*

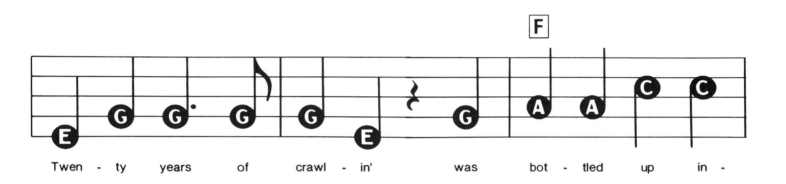

pin drop when Tommy stopped and   blocked the door.

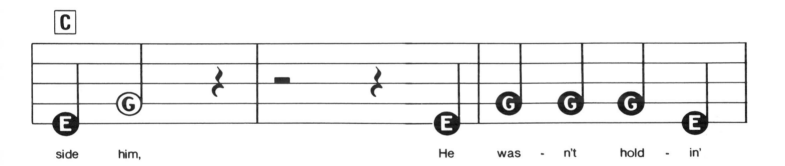

Twen - ty   years   of   crawl - in'   was   bot - tled   up   in -

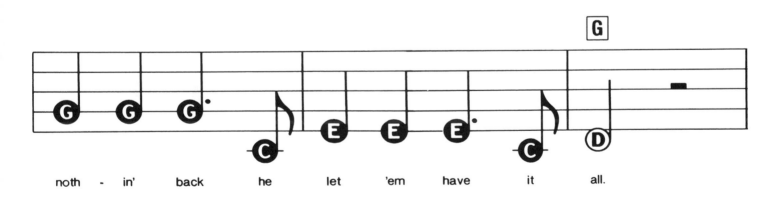

side   him,   He   was - n't   hold - in'

noth - in'   back   he   let   'em   have   it   all.

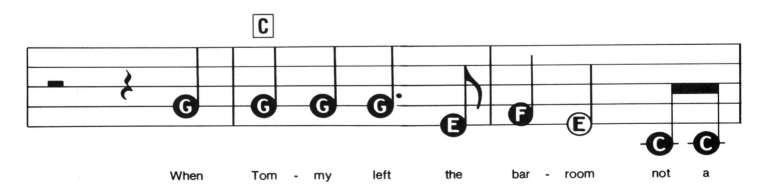

When   Tom - my   left   the   bar - room   not   a

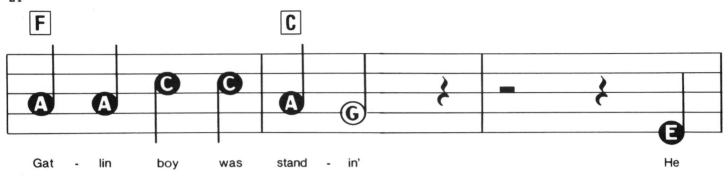

Gat - lin boy was stand - in' He

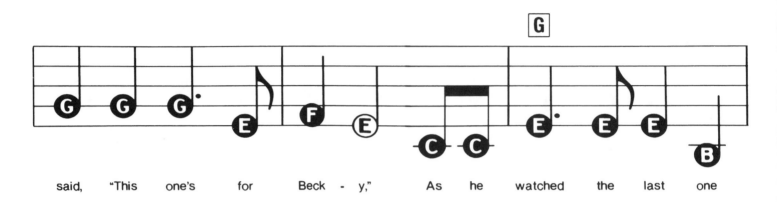

said, "This one's for Beck - y," As he watched the last one

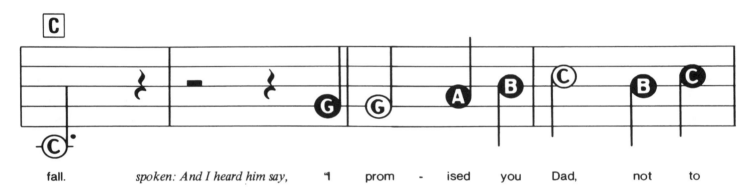

fall. *spoken: And I heard him say,* "I prom - ised you Dad, not to

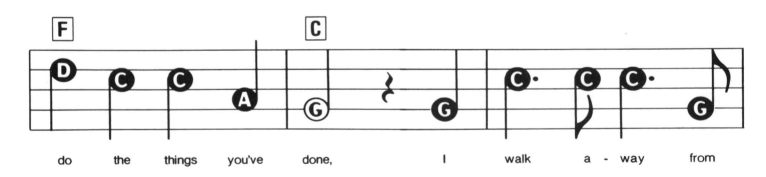

do the things you've done, I walk a - way from

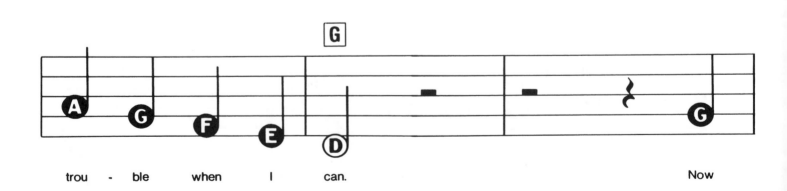

trou - ble when I can. Now

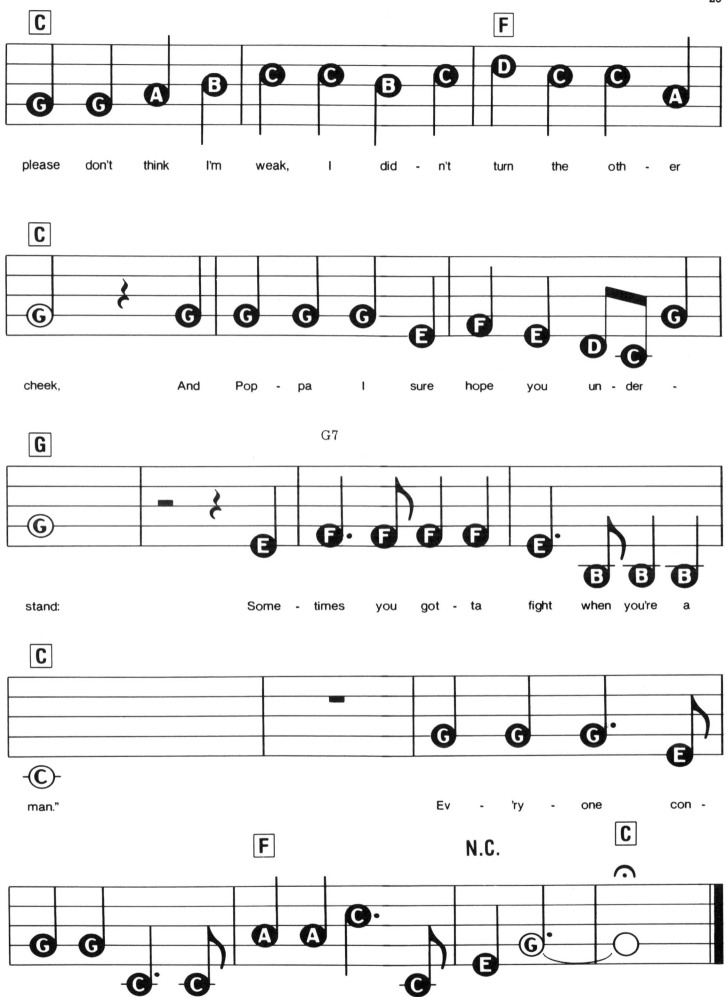

Crazy Arms

Registration 2
Rhythm: Country Rock or Fox Trot

Words and Music by Ralph Mooney
and Charles Seals

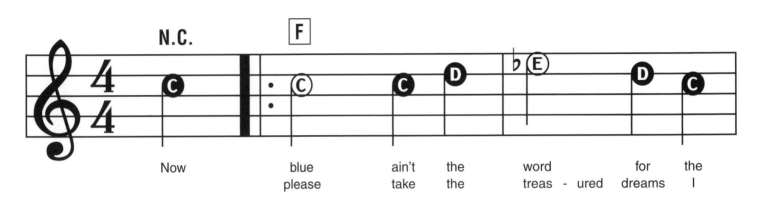

Now / please
blue / take
ain't / the
the / treas - ured
word / dreams
for / I
the

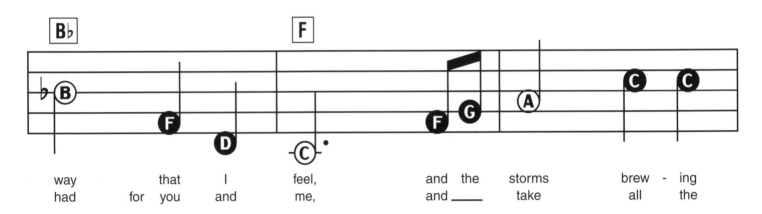

way / had
that / for
I / you
and
feel, / me,
and / and
the / storms / take
brew / all
ing / the

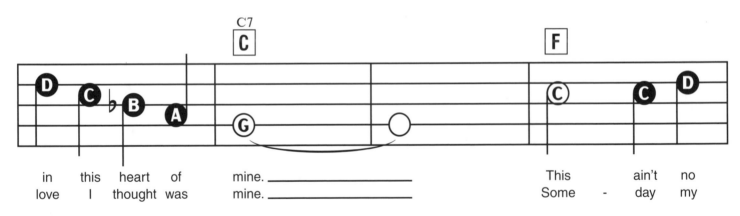

in / love
this / I
heart / thought
of / was
mine. / mine.

This / Some - day
ain't / my
no

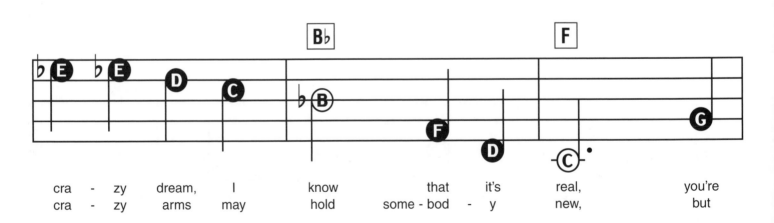

cra / cra
zy / zy
dream, / arms
I / may
know / hold
that / some - bod
it's / y
real, / new,
you're / but

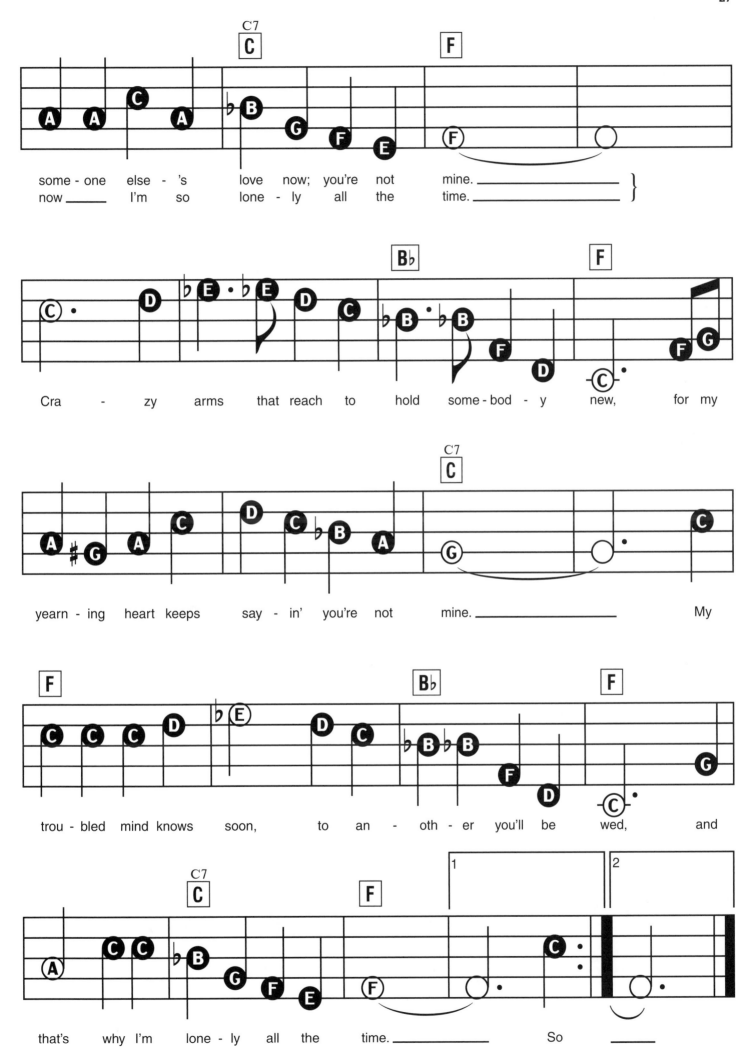

Daddy Don't You Walk So Fast

Registration 4
Rhythm: Country or Swing

Words and Music by Peter Callender
and Geoff Stephens

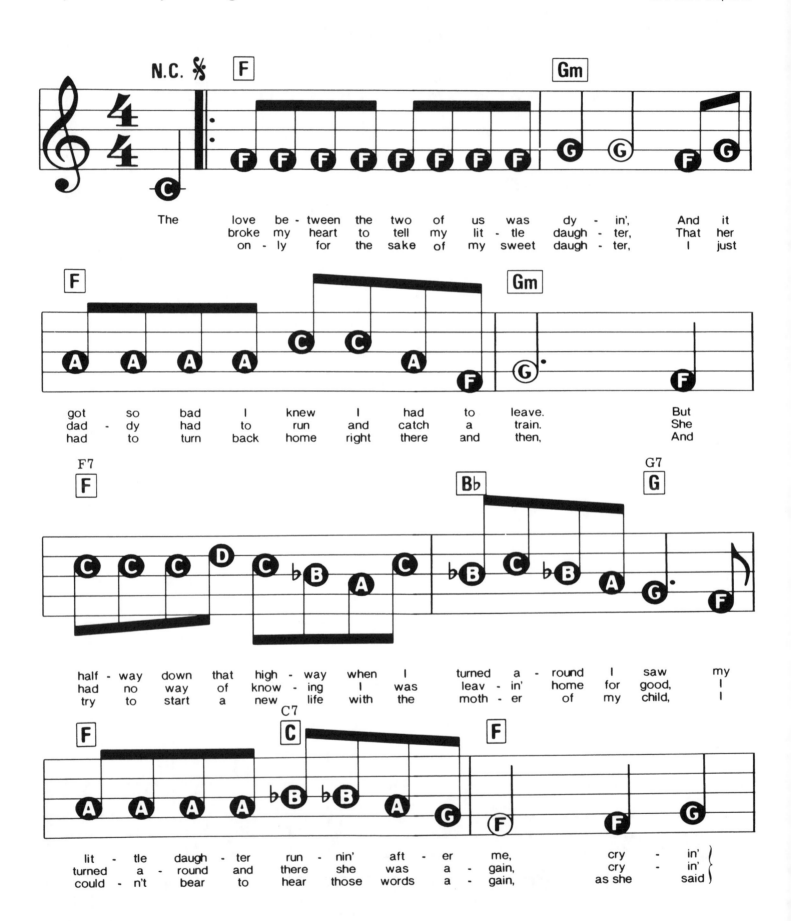

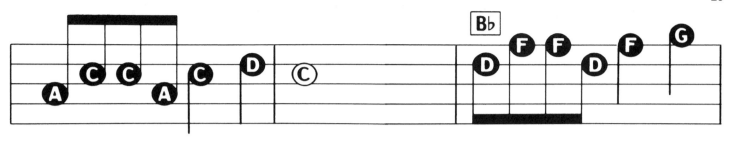

"Dad - dy don't you walk so fast, Dad - dy don't you walk so

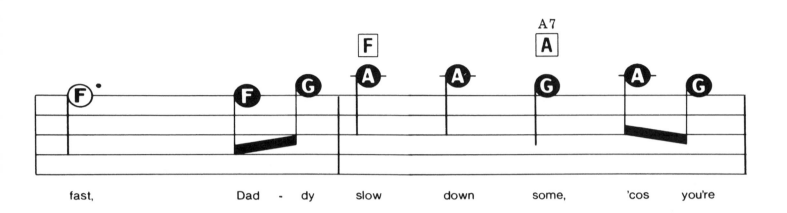

fast, Dad - dy slow down some, 'cos you're

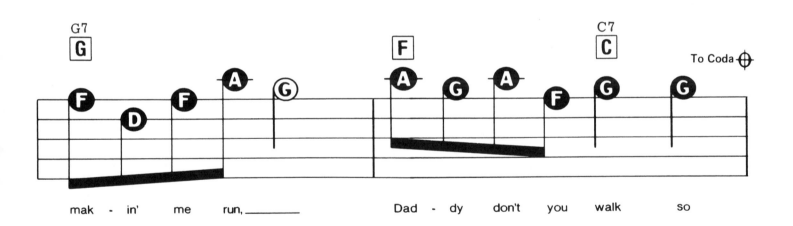

mak - in' me run, _____ Dad - dy don't you walk so

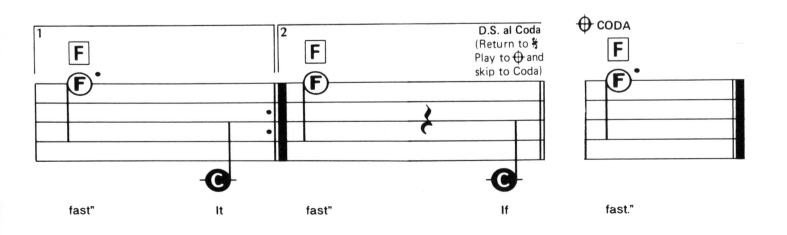

fast" It fast" If fast."

D-I-V-O-R-C-E

Registration 2
Rhythm: Country

Words and Music by Bobby Braddock
and Curly Putman

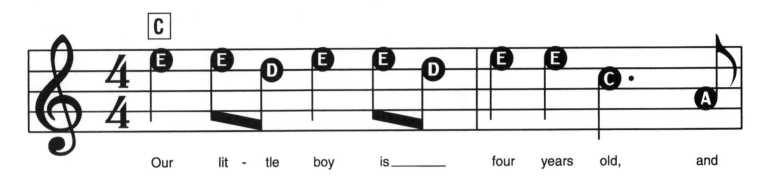

Our lit - tle boy is _____ four years old, and

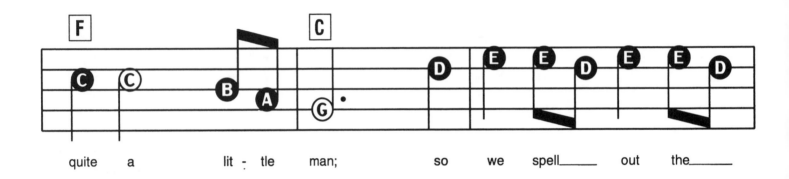

quite a lit - tle man; so we spell _____ out the _____

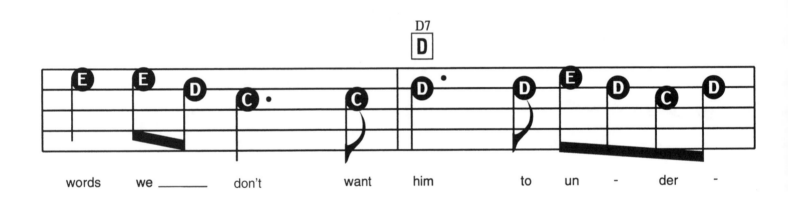

words we _____ don't want him to un - der -

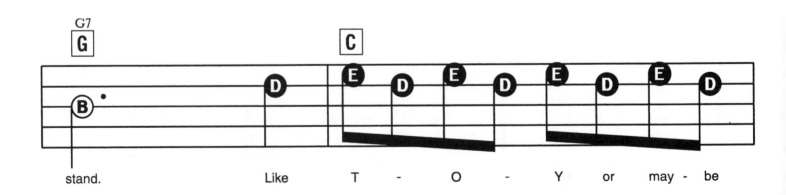

stand. Like T - O - Y or may - be

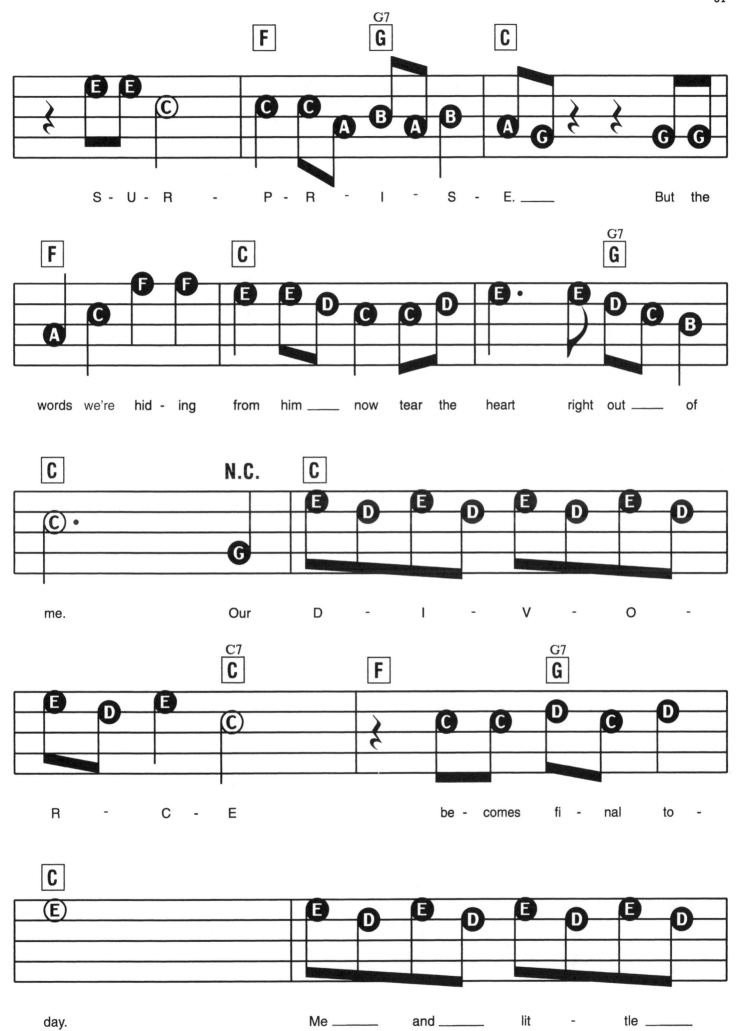

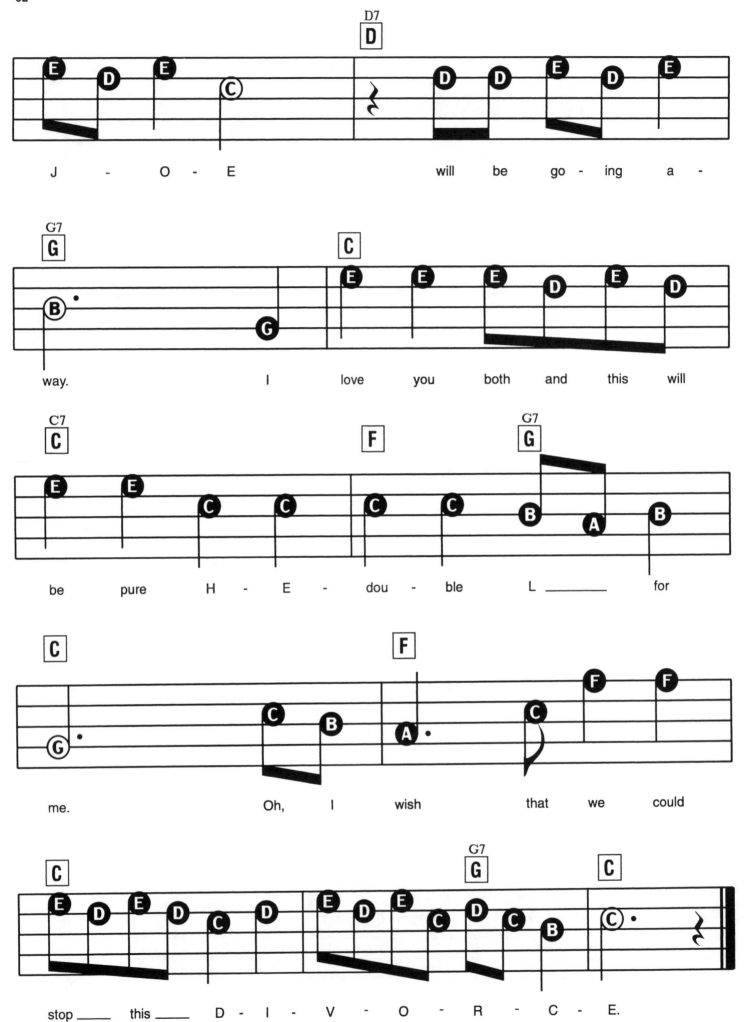

Drivin' My Life Away

Registration 8
Rhythm: Country Rock or Fox Trot

Words and Music by Eddie Rabbitt,
Even Stevens and David Malloy

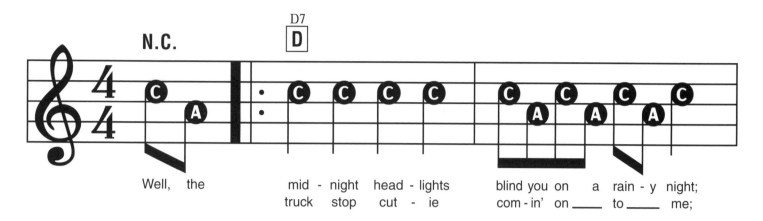

Well, the   mid - night head - lights   blind you on   a   rain - y night;
        truck stop cut - ie   com - in' on ___ to ___ me;

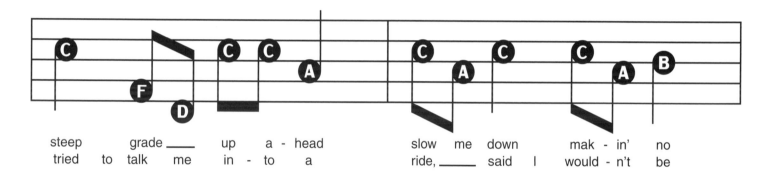

steep grade ___ up a - head   slow me down   mak - in' no
tried to talk me in - to a   ride, ___ said I would - n't be

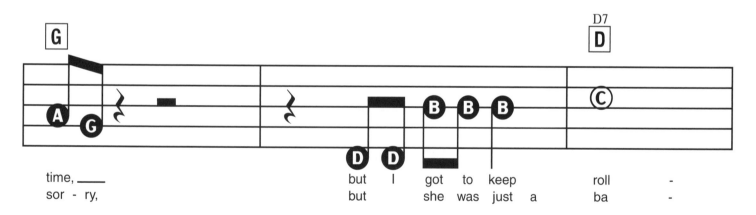

time, ___   but I got to keep   roll -
sor - ry,   but she was just a   ba -

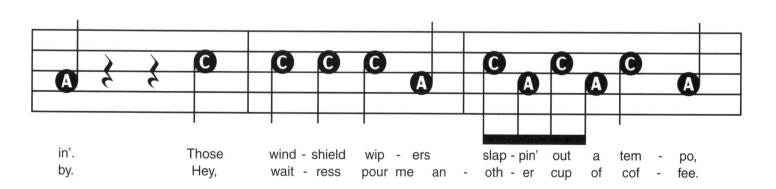

in'.   Those wind - shield wip - ers   slap - pin' out a tem - po,
by.   Hey, wait - ress pour me an - oth - er cup of cof - fee.

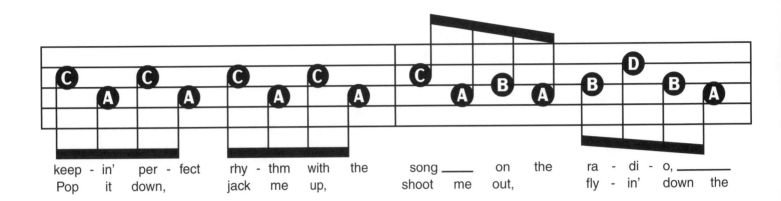

keep - in' per - fect rhy - thm with the song ___ on the ra - di - o, ___
Pop it down, jack me up, shoot me out, fly - in' down the

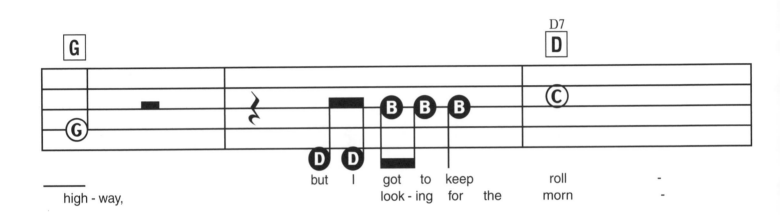

G | | | D7 / D

___ high - way,
but I got to keep look - ing for the roll morn

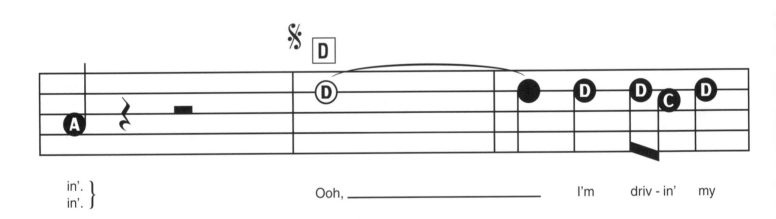

D

in'. / in'.
Ooh, ___ I'm driv - in' my

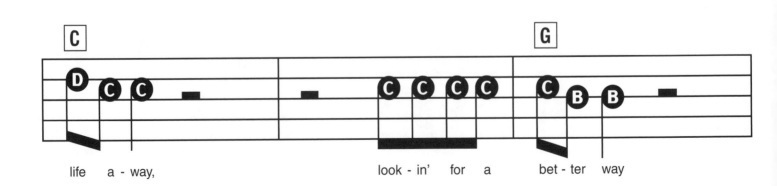

C | | | G

life a - way, look - in' for a bet - ter way

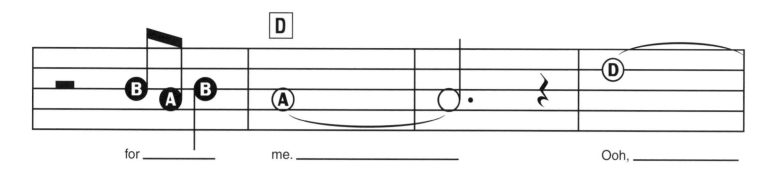

for _____ me. _____ Ooh, _____

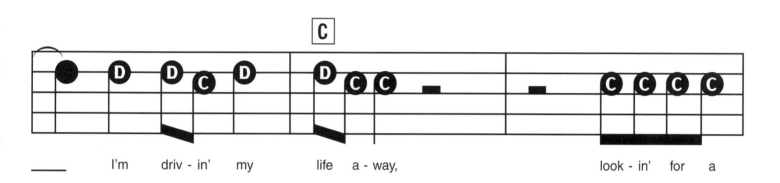

____ I'm driv - in' my life a - way, look - in' for a

To Coda ⊕

1

2

D.S. al Coda
(Return to 𝄋
Play to ⊕ and
Skip to Coda)

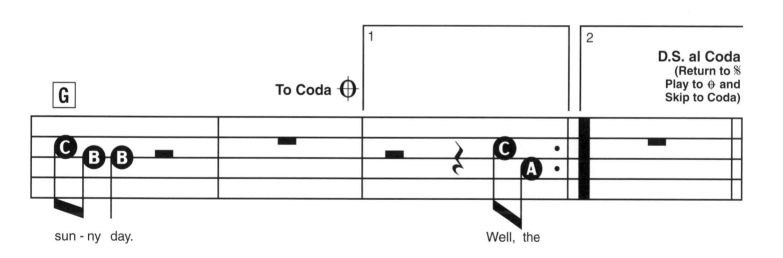

sun - ny day. Well, the

CODA
⊕

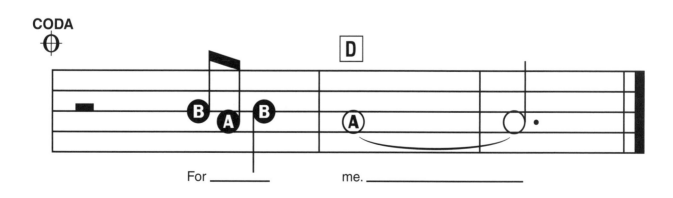

For _____ me. _____

Dream Baby
(How Long Must I Dream)

Registration 7
Rhythm: Ballad or Fox Trot

Words and Music by
Cindy Walker

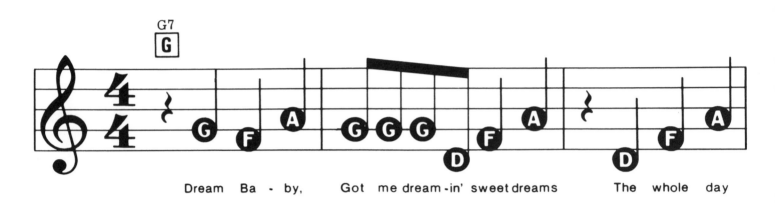

Dream Ba - by, Got me dream-in' sweet dreams The whole day

through. Dream Ba - by, Got me dream-in' sweet dreams Night time

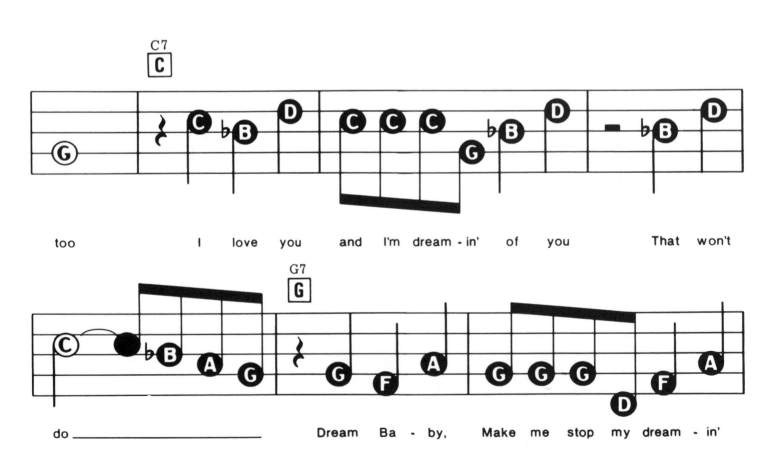

too I love you and I'm dream-in' of you That won't

do _____ Dream Ba - by, Make me stop my dream-in'

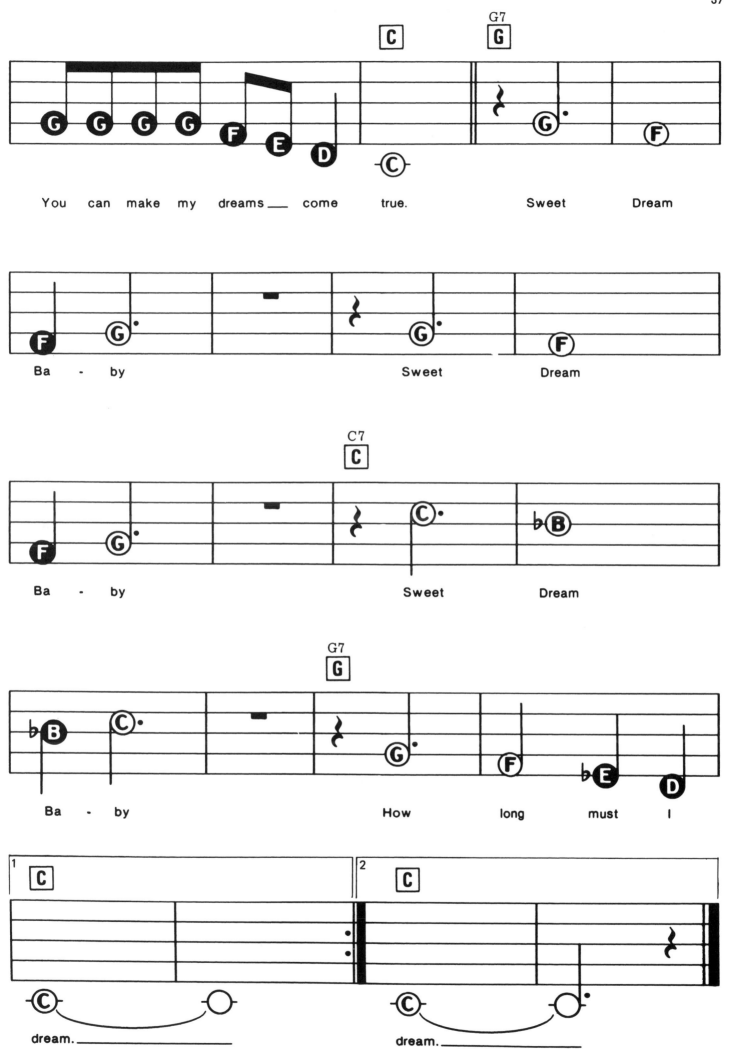

Duelin' Banjos

Registration 10
Rhythm: 4/4 March

By Arthur Smith

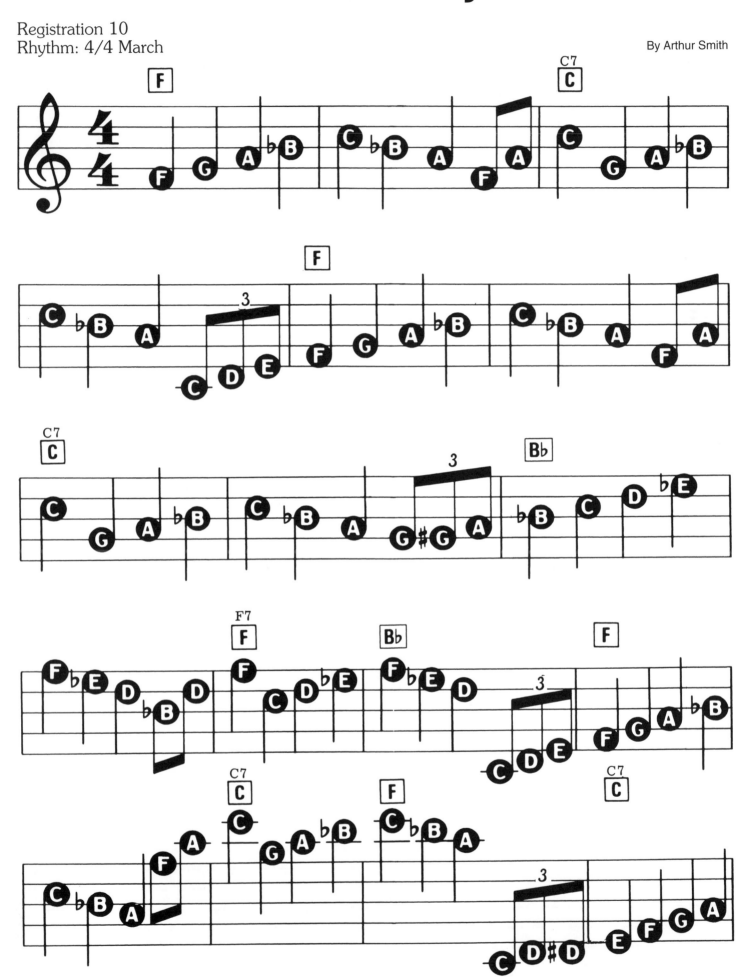

39

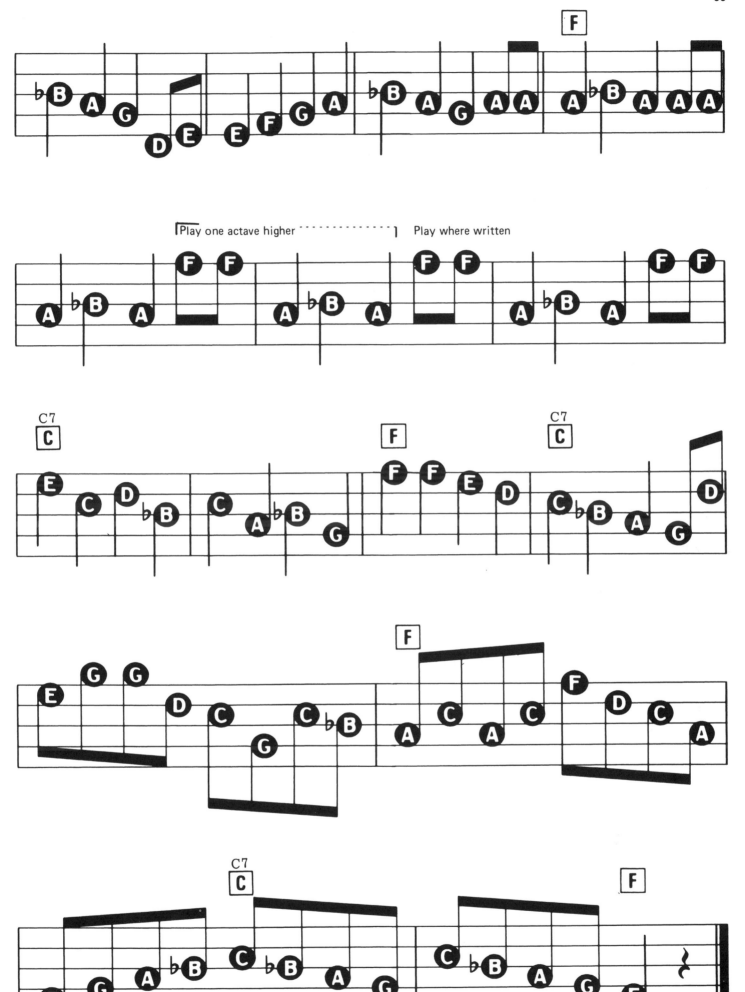

Easy Loving

Registration 3
Rhythm: Ballad or Slow Rock

Words and Music by
Freddie Hart

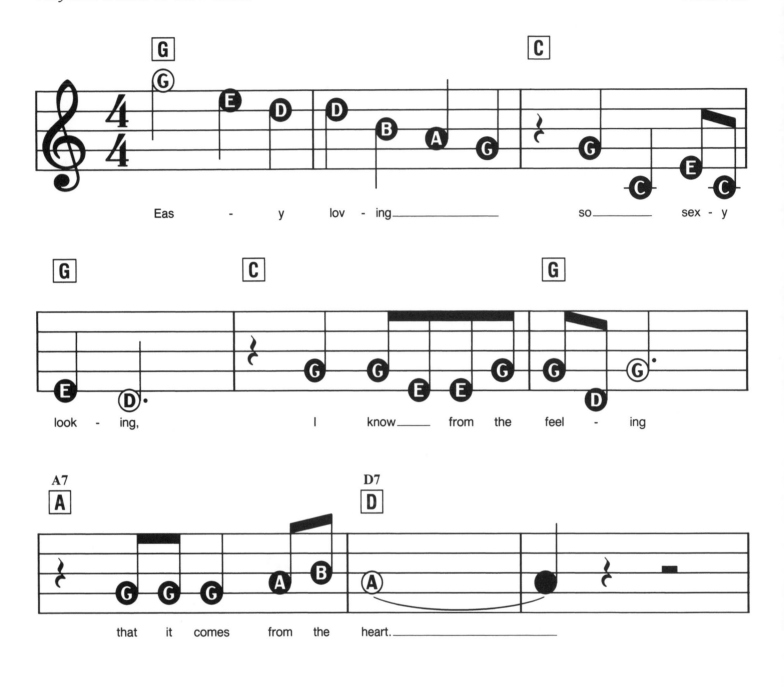

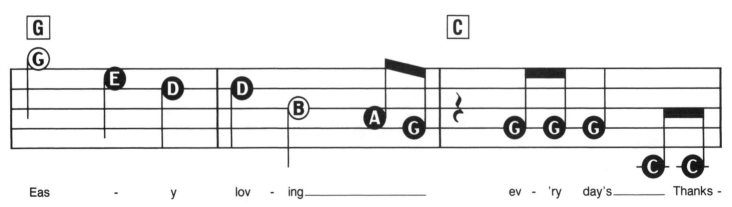

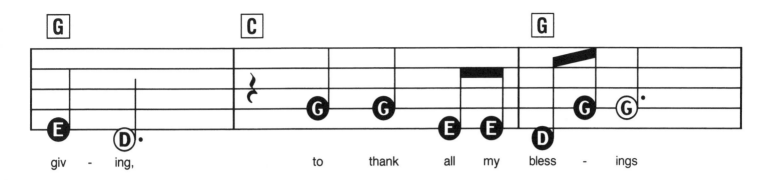

giv - ing, to thank all my bless - ings

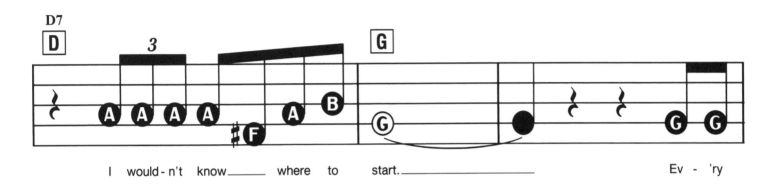

I would - n't know_____ where to start._____ Ev - 'ry

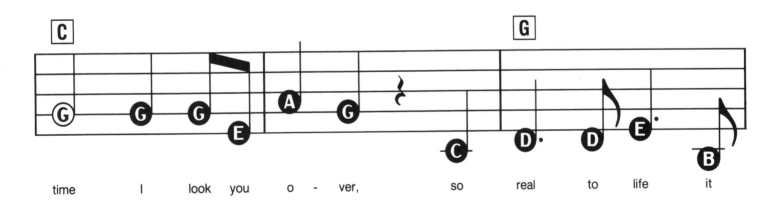

time I look you o - ver, so real to life it

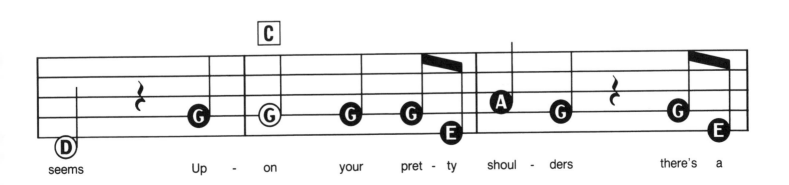

seems Up - on your pret - ty shoul - ders there's a

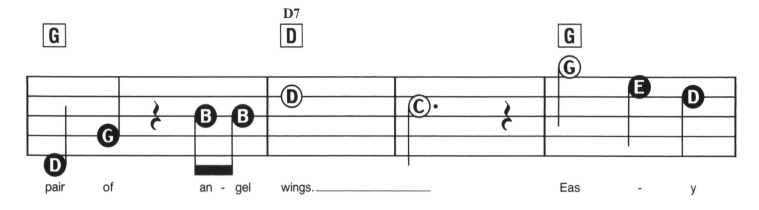

pair   of   an - gel   wings._____   Eas - y

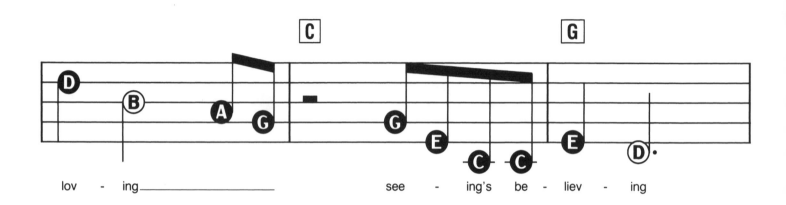

lov - ing_____   see - ing's be - liev - ing

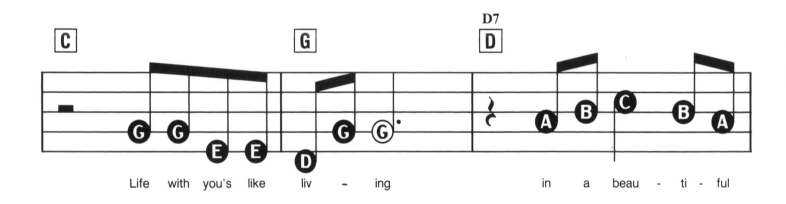

Life   with   you's   like   liv – ing   in   a   beau - ti - ful

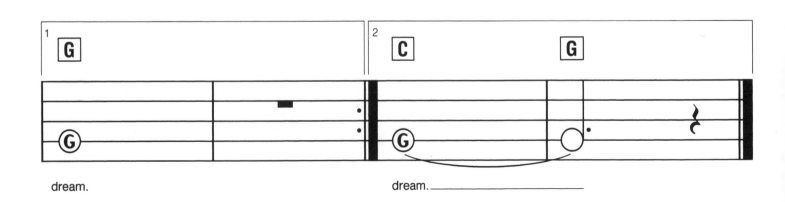

dream.   dream._____

Family Tradition

Registration 8
Rhythm: Country or Rock

Words and Music by
Hank Williams, Jr.

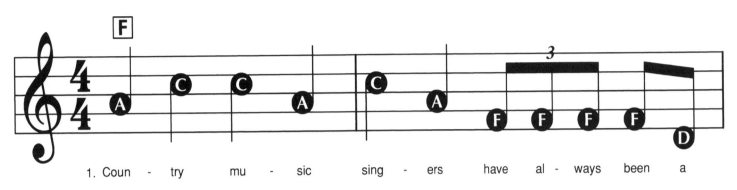

1. Coun - try mu - sic sing - ers have al - ways been a

2. 3. *(See additional lyrics)*

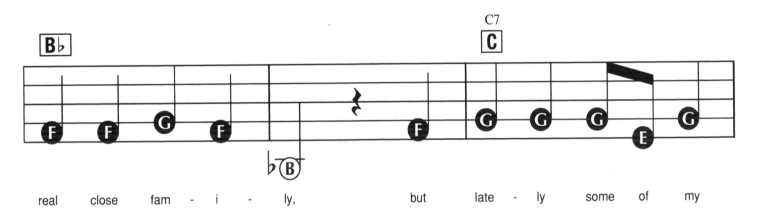

real close fam - i - ly, but late - ly some of my

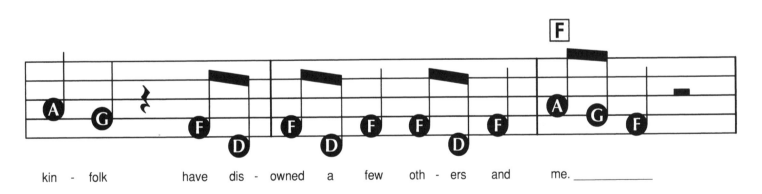

kin - folk have dis - owned a few oth - ers and me. _____

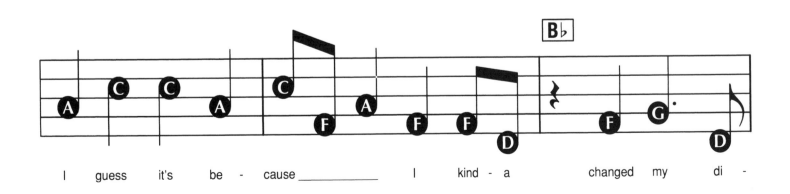

I guess it's be - cause _____ I kind - a changed my di -

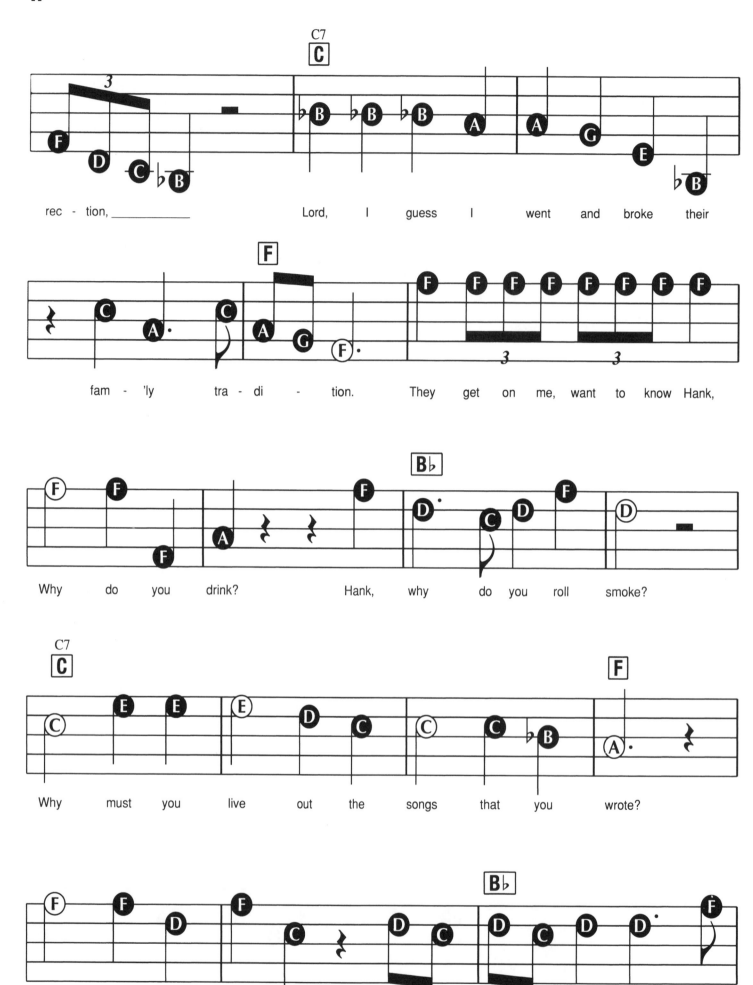

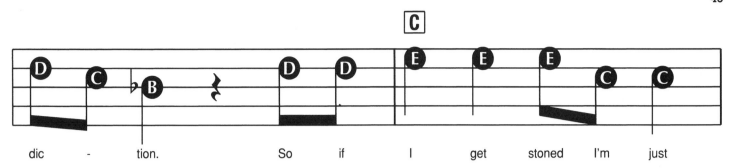

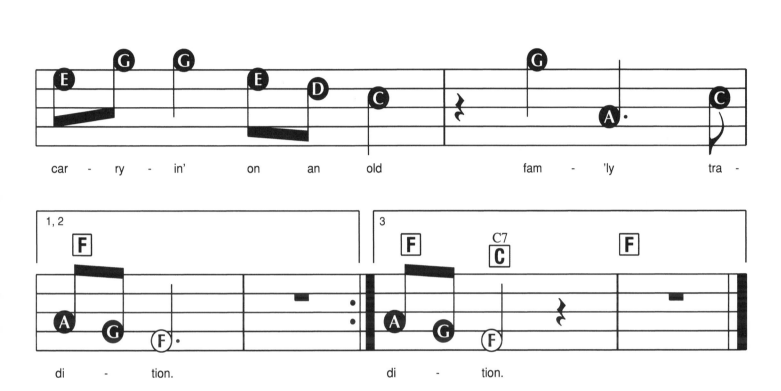

Additional Lyrics

2. I am very proud of my daddy's name,
Although his kind of music and mine ain't exactly the same
Stop and think it over put yourself in my position
If I get stoned and sing all night long, it's a family tradition.

Chorus 2: So don't ask me Hank
Why do you drink?
Hank, why do you roll smoke?
Why must you live out the songs that you wrote?
If I'm down in a honky tonk, some old slicks tryin' to give me friction
I say leave me alone, I'm singin' all night long, it's a family tradition.

3. Lordy, I have loved some ladies and I have loved Jim Beam
And they both tried to kill me in Nineteen Seventy Three
When that doctor asked me, Son, how'd you get in this condition?
I said hey saw bones I'm just carryin' on an old family tradition.

Chorus 3: So don't ask me Hank
Why do you drink?
Hank, why do you roll smoke?
Why must you live out the songs that you wrote?
Stop and think it over, try to put yourself in my unique position
If I get stoned and sing all night long, it's a family tradition.

Feels So Right

Registration 9
Rhythm: Slow Rock or Ballad

Words and Music by
Randy Owen

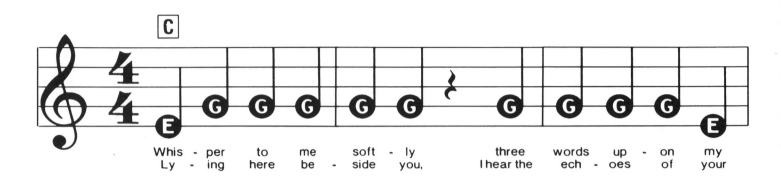

Whis - per to me soft - ly three words up - on my
Ly - ing here be - side you, I hear the ech - oes of your

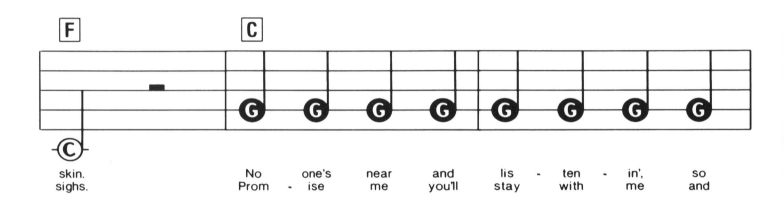

skin. No one's near and lis - ten - in', so
sighs. Prom - ise me and you'll stay with me and

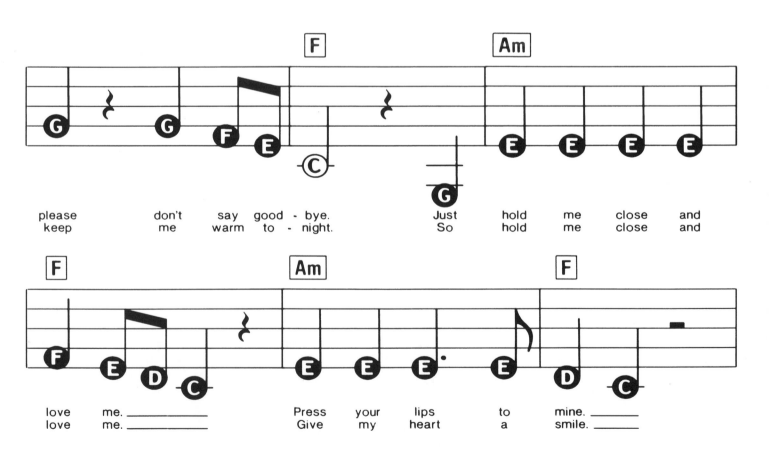

please don't say good - bye. Just hold me close and
keep me warm to - night. So hold me close and

love me. _____ Press your lips to mine. _____
love me. _____ Give my heart a smile. _____

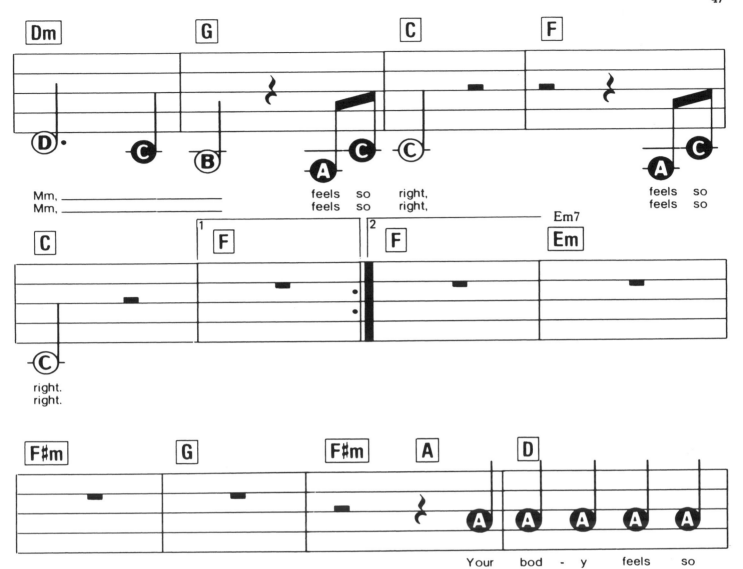

Mm, _____
Mm, _____

feels so right,
feels so right,

feels so
feels so

right.
right.

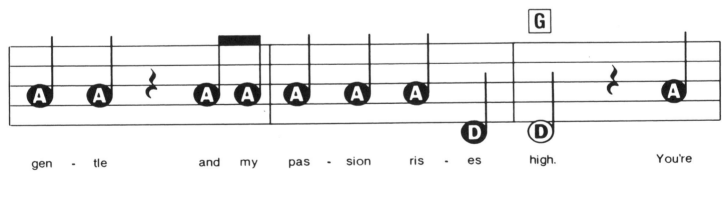

Your bod - y feels so

gen - tle   and my pas - sion ris - es high.   You're

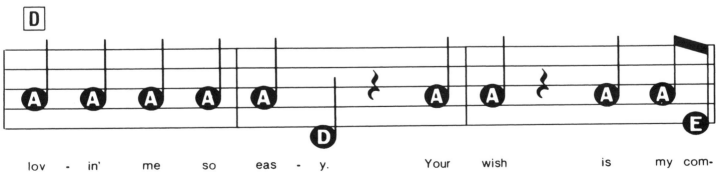

lov - in' me so eas - y.   Your wish is my com-

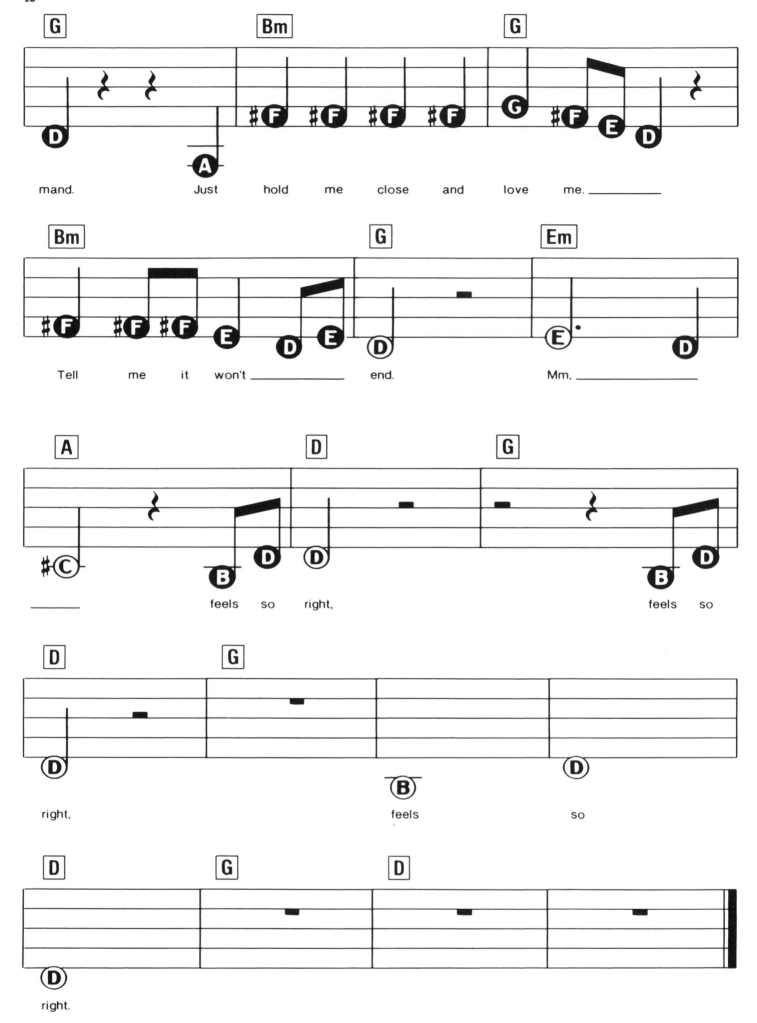

For the Good Times

Registration 2
Rhythm: Country or Swing

Words and Music by
Kris Kristofferson

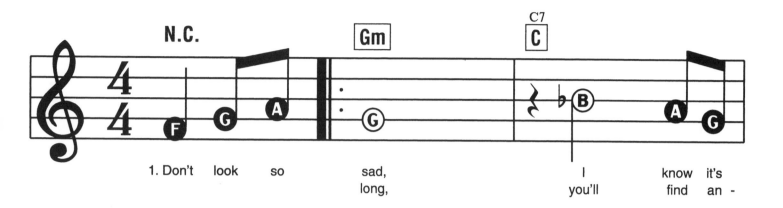

1. Don't look so sad, sad, / long, I know it's / you'll find an -

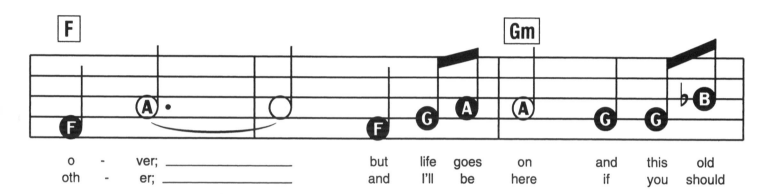

o - ver; _____ but life goes on and this old
oth - er; _____ and I'll be on here if you should

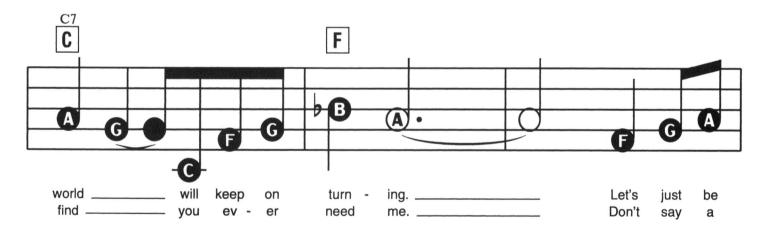

world _____ will keep on turn - ing. _____ Let's just be
find _____ you ev - er need me. _____ Don't say a

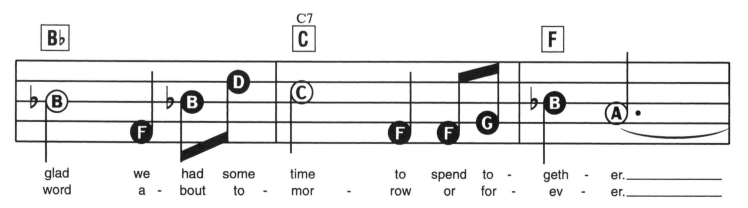

glad we had some time to spend to - geth - er. _____
word a - bout to - mor - row or for - ev - er. _____

There's no need to watch the
There'll be time e - nough for

bridg - es that we're burn - ing.
sad - ness when you leave me.
Lay your

head up - on my pil - low,

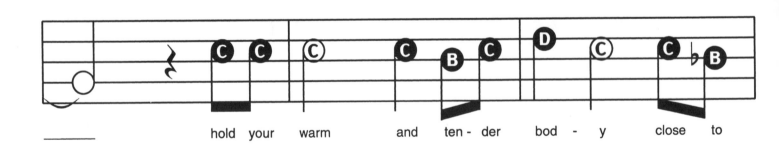

hold your warm and ten - der bod - y close to

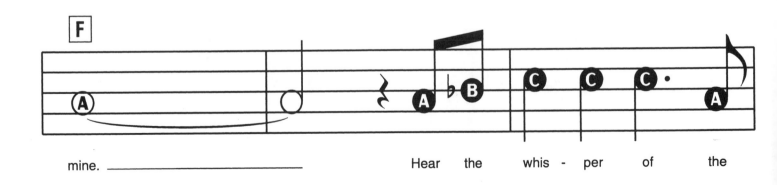

mine. Hear the whis - per of the

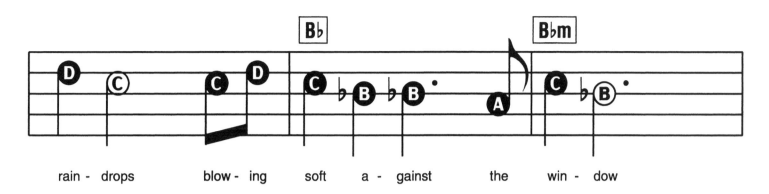

rain - drops   blow - ing   soft   a - gainst   the   win - dow

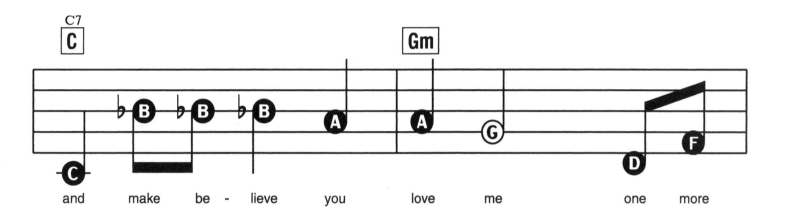

and   make   be - lieve   you   love   me   one   more

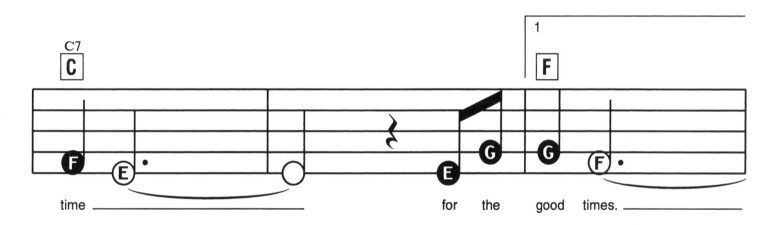

time _____   for   the   good   times. _____

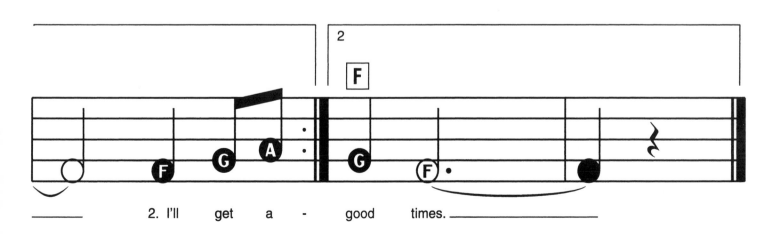

_____   2. I'll   get   a -   good   times. _____

Folsom Prison Blues

Registration 3
Rhythm: Rock or Fox Trot

Words and Music by
John R. Cash

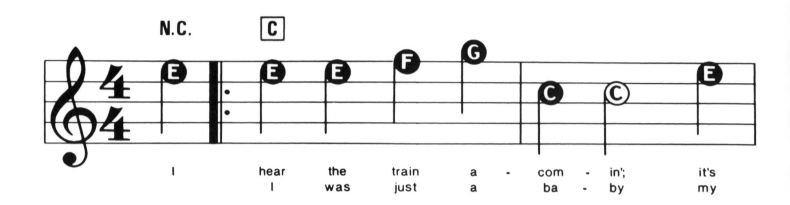

I hear the train a - com - in'; it's
I was just a ba - by my

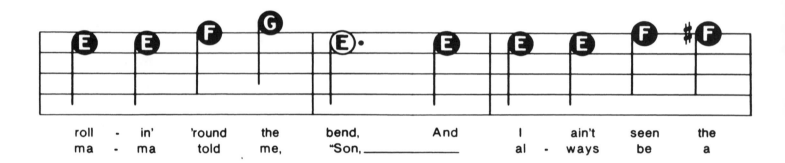

roll - in' 'round the bend, And I ain't seen the
ma - ma told me, "Son,____ al - ways be a

sun - shine since I don't know when. I'm
good boy; since don't ever play with guns. But I

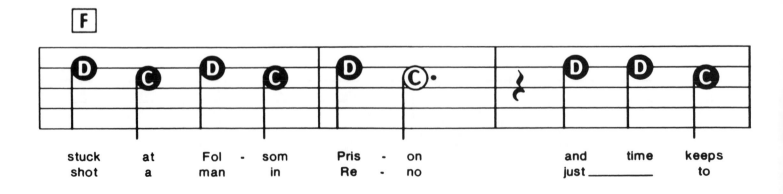

stuck at Fol - som Pris - on and time keeps
shot a man in Re - no just____ to

53

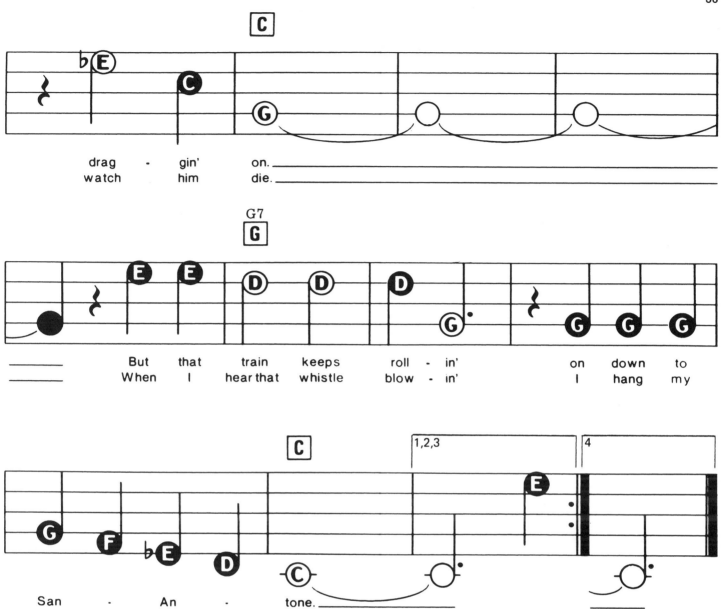

3. I bet there's rich folks eatin' in a fancy dining car.
   They're prob'ly drinkin' coffee and smokin' big cigars,
   But I know I had it comin', I know I can't be free,
   But those people keep a-movin', and that's what tortures me.

4. Well, if they freed me from this prison, if that railroad train was mine,
   I bet I'd move over a little farther down the line,
   Far from Folsom Prison, that's where I want to stay.
   And I'd let that lonesome whistle blow my blues away.

From Graceland to the Promised Land

Registration 4
Rhythm: Country or Swing

Words and Music by
Merle Haggard

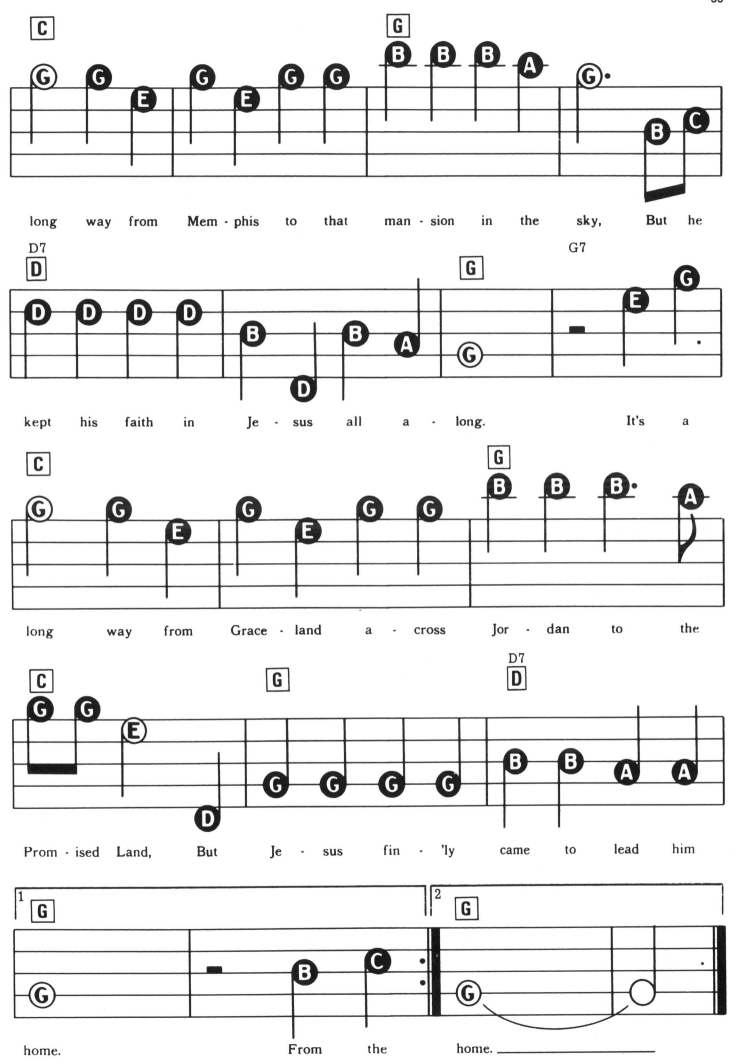

Gentle on My Mind

Registration 10
Rhythm: Fox Trot or Pops

Words and Music by
John Hartford

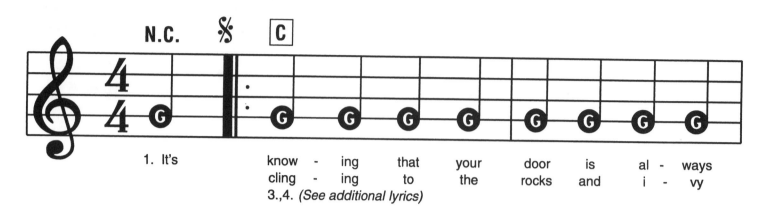

1. It's know - ing that your door is al - ways
cling - ing to the rocks and i - vy
3.,4. *(See additional lyrics)*

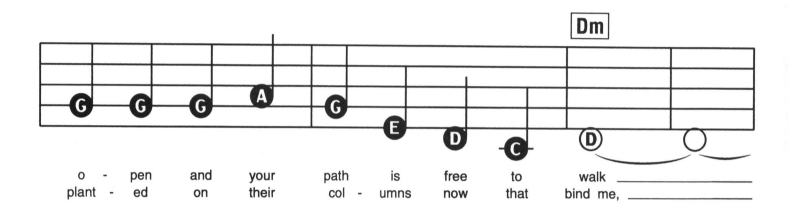

o - pen and your path is free to walk _____
plant - ed on their col - umns free now to that bind me, _____

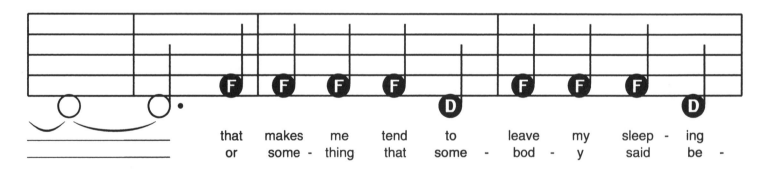

that makes me tend to leave my sleep - ing
or some - thing that some - bod - y said be -

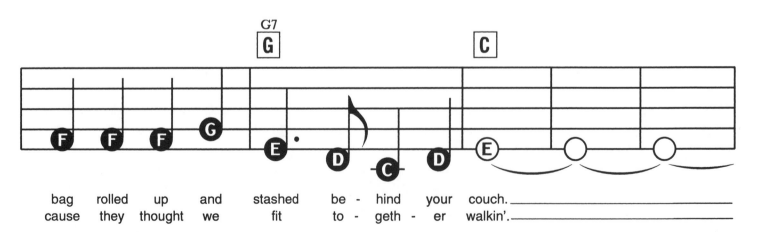

bag rolled up and stashed be - hind your couch. _____
cause they thought we fit to - geth - er walkin'. _____

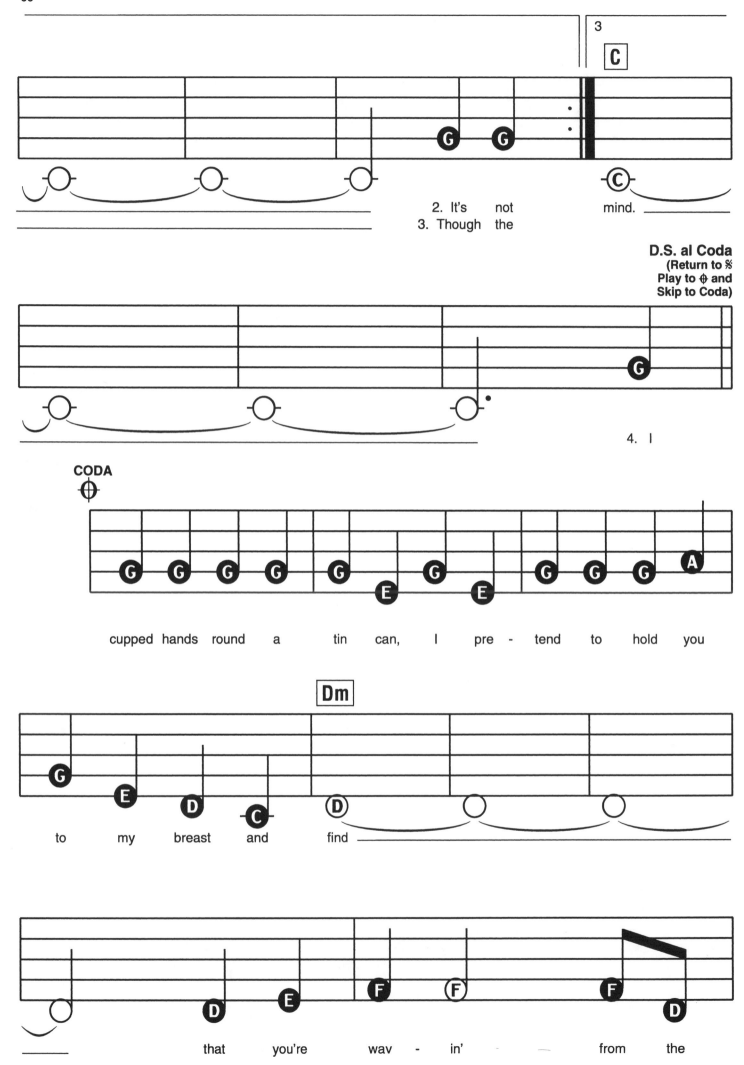

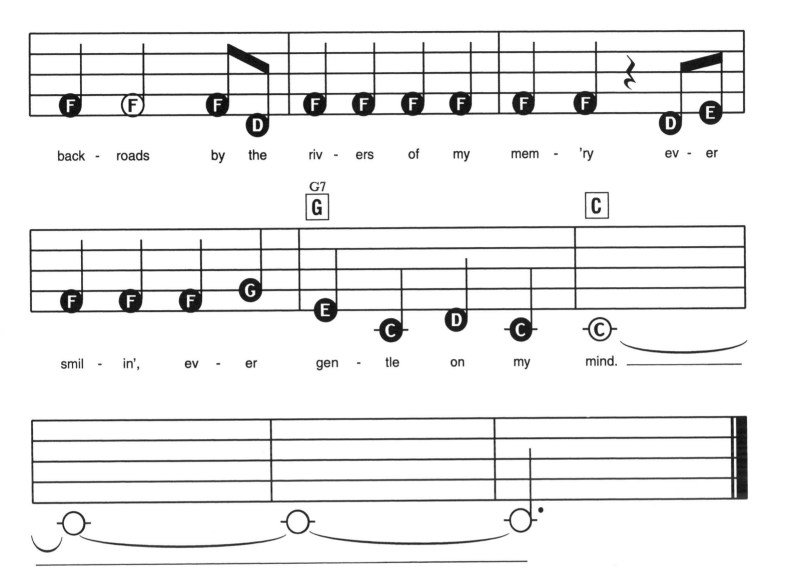

back - roads   by   the   riv - ers   of   my   mem - 'ry   ev - er

smil - in',   ev - er   gen - tle   on   my   mind. _____

Additional Lyrics

3. Though the wheat fields and the clotheslines
   and the junkyards and the highways come between us,
   and some other woman cryin' to her mother
   'cause she turned and I was gone.
   I still might run in silence,
   tears of joy might stain my face,
   and the summer sun might burn me till I'm blind,
   but not to where I cannot see you
   walkin' on the backroads
   by the rivers flowing gentle on my mind.

4. I dip my cup of soup back from some gurglin',
   cracklin' cauldron in some train yard,
   my beard a rough'ning coal pile and
   a dirty hat pulled low across my face.
   Through cupped hands round a tin can,
   I pretend to hold you to my breast and find
   that you're wavin' from the backroads
   by the rivers of my mem'ry,
   ever smilin', ever gentle on my mind.

Good Woman Blues

Registration 8
Rhythm: Country Rock or Fox Trot

Words and Music by
Ken McDuffie

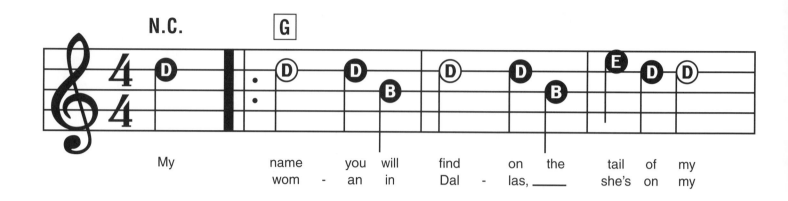

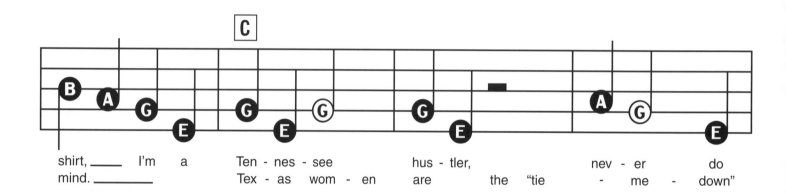

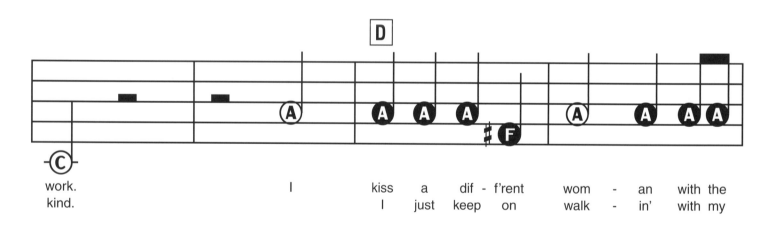

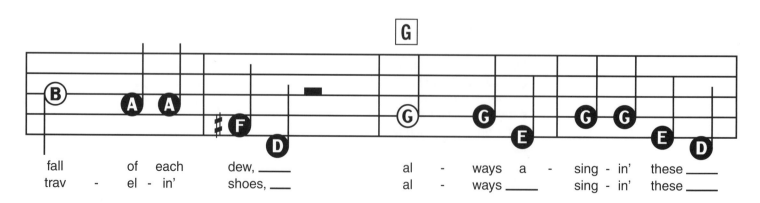

61

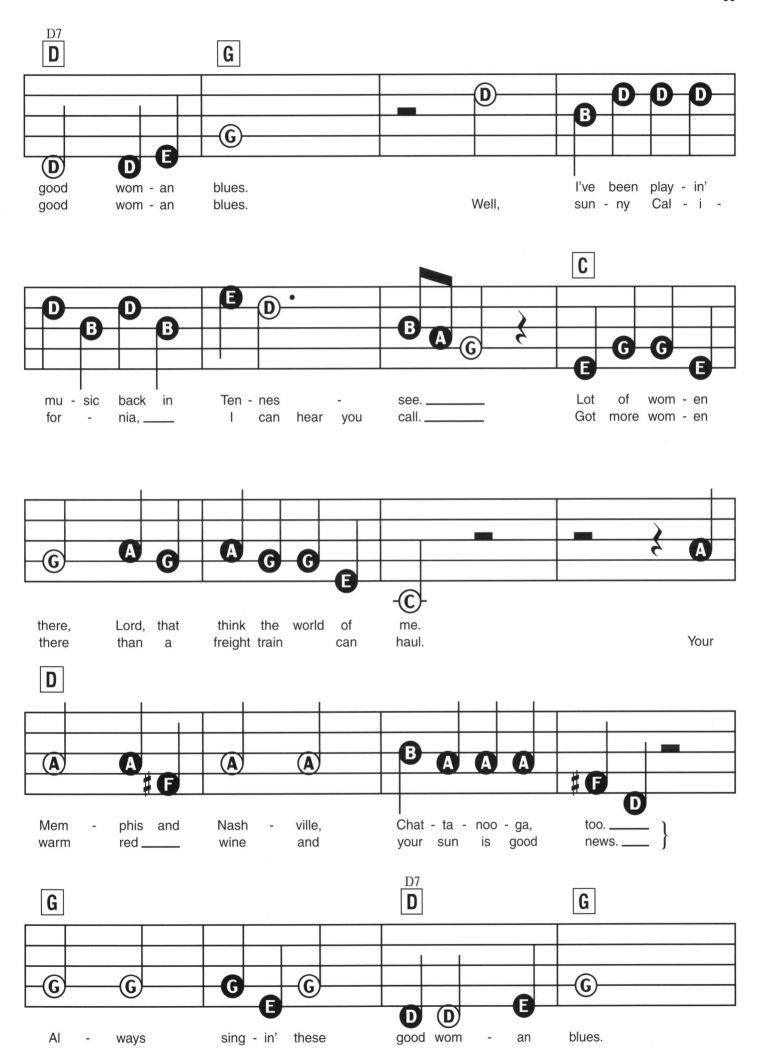

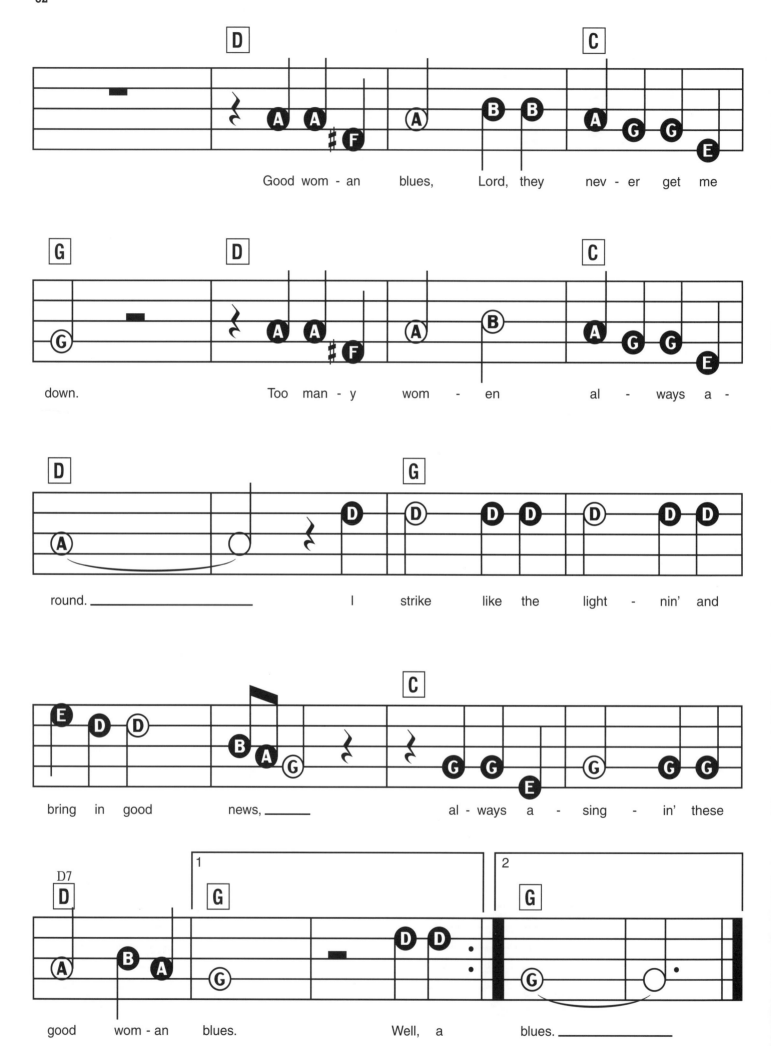

He'll Have to Go

Registration 5
Rhythm: Waltz

Words and Music by Joe Allison
and Audrey Allison

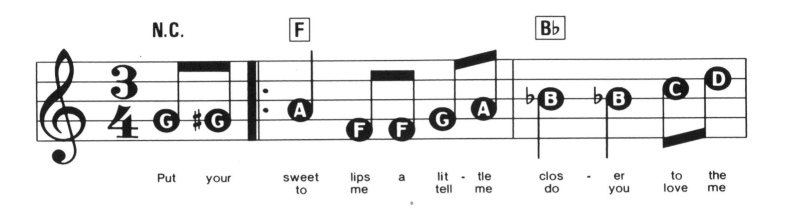

Put your sweet lips a lit-tle clos-er to the
to me tell me do you love me

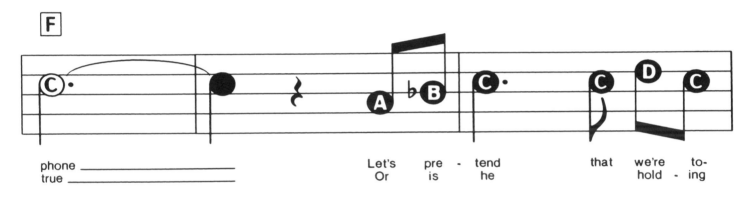

phone _____
true _____
Let's pre - tend that we're to-
Or is he hold - ing

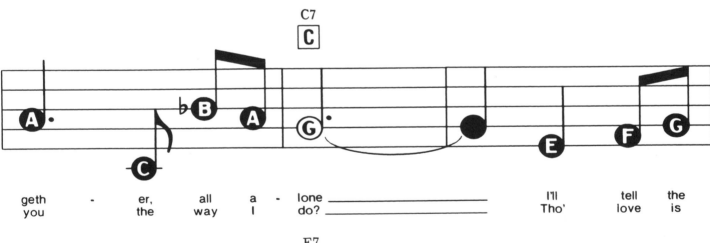

geth - er, all a - lone _____ I'll tell the
you the way I do? Tho' love is

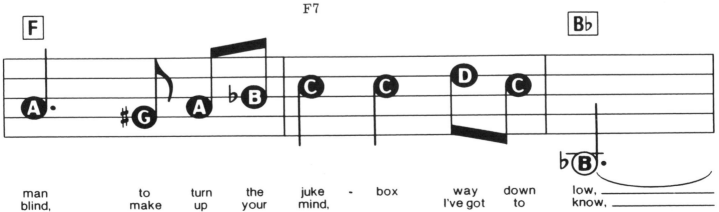

man to turn the juke - box way down low,
blind, make up your mind, I've got to know,

64

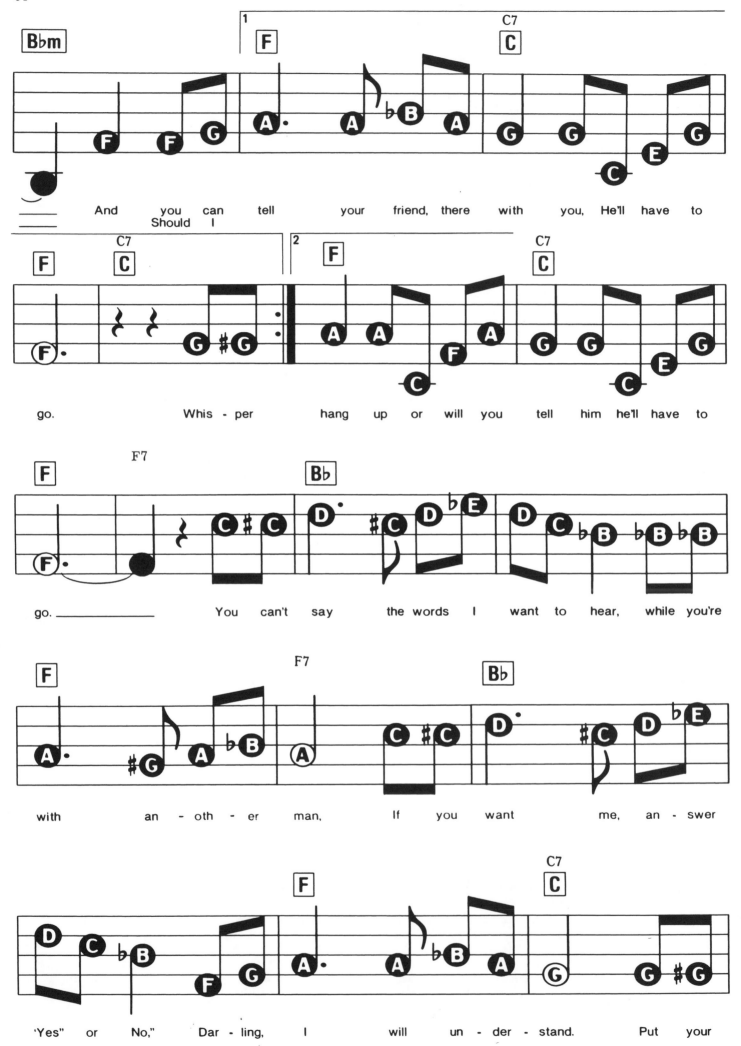

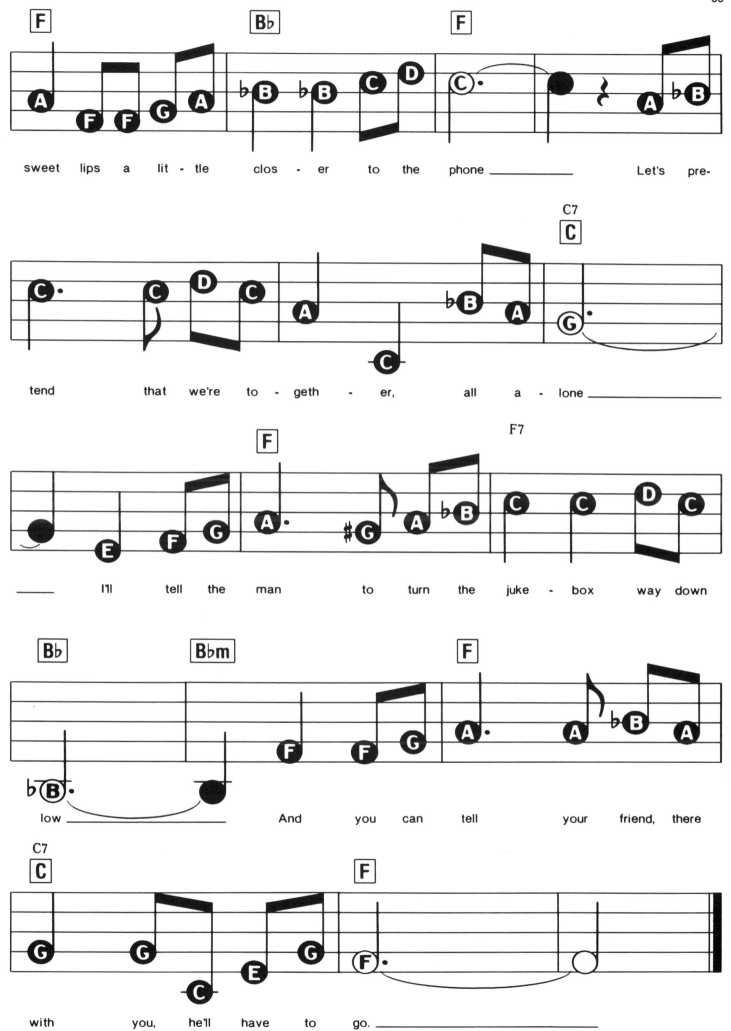

Hello Darlin'

Registration 8
Rhythm: Waltz

Words and Music by
Conway Twitty

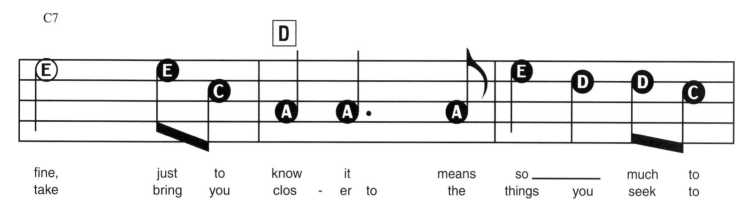

fine,   just   to   know   it   means   so _____ much   to

take   bring   you   clos - er   to   the   things   you   seek   to

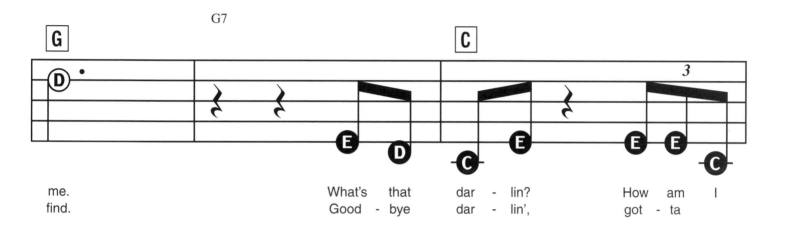

me.   What's   that   dar - lin?   How   am   I

find.   Good - bye   dar - lin',   got - ta

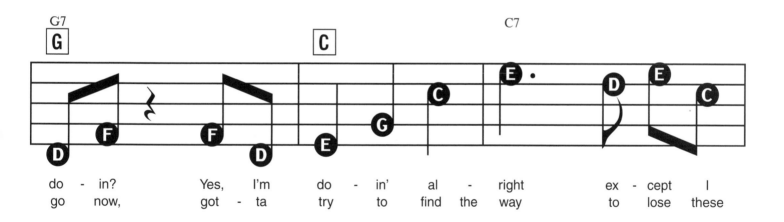

do - in?   Yes,   I'm   do - in'   al - right   ex - cept   I

go   now,   got - ta   try   to   find   the   way   to   lose   these

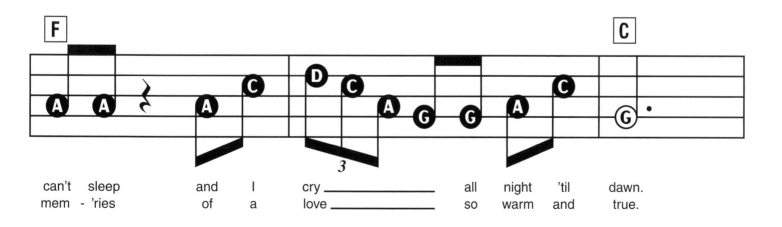

can't sleep   and   I   cry _____ all   night   'til   dawn.

mem - 'ries   of   a   love _____ so   warm   and   true.

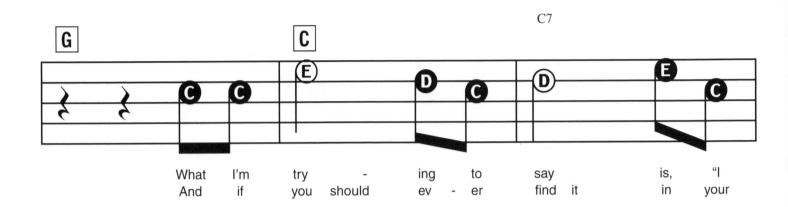

What I'm try - ing to say is, "I
And if you should ev - er find it in your

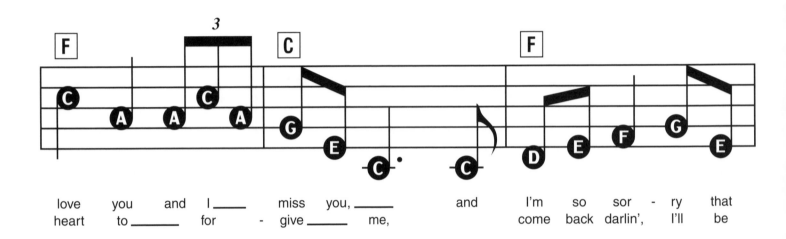

love you and I ____ miss you, ____ and I'm so sor - ry that
heart to ____ for - give ____ me, come back darlin', I'll be

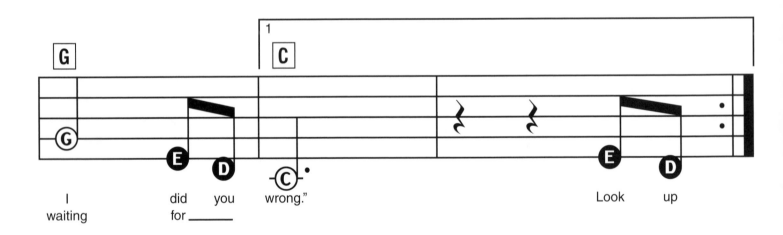

I did you wrong." Look up
waiting for ____

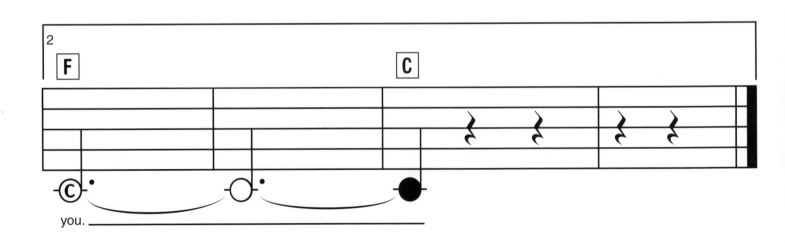

you. ____

Honey
(Open That Door)

Registration 1
Rhythm: Country or Shuffle

Words and Music by
Mel Tillis

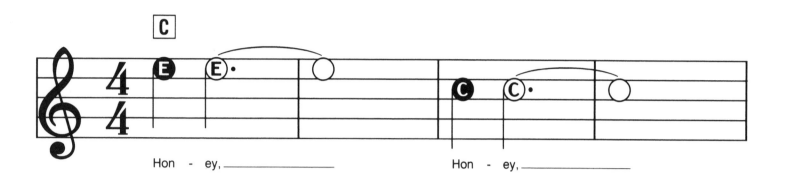

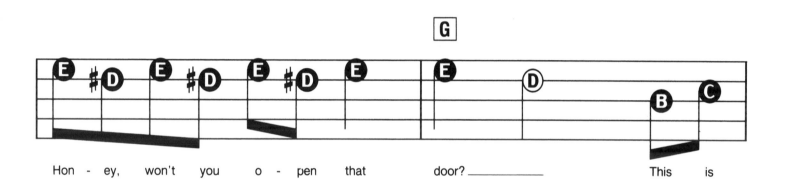

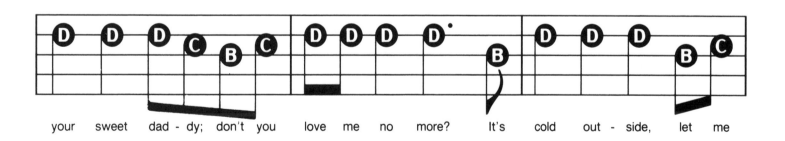

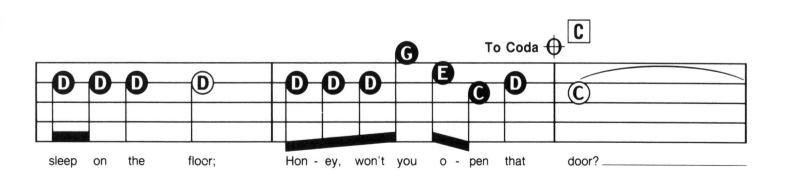

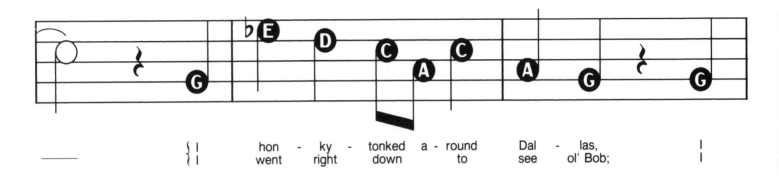

I honk-y - tonked a - round Dal - las, I
went right down to see ol' Bob;

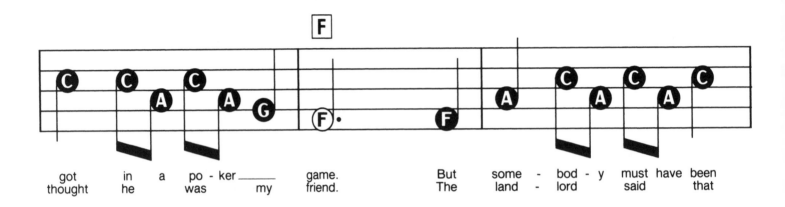

got in a po - ker ____ game. But some - bod - y must have been
thought he was my friend. The land - lord said that

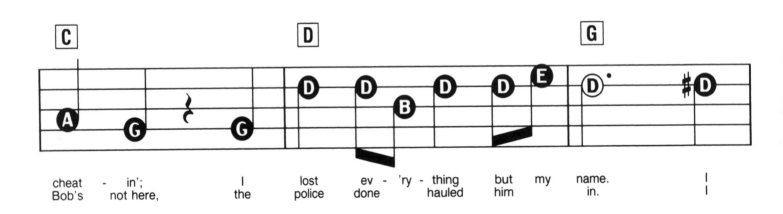

cheat - in'; I lost ev - 'ry - thing but my name. I
Bob's not here, the police done hauled him in.

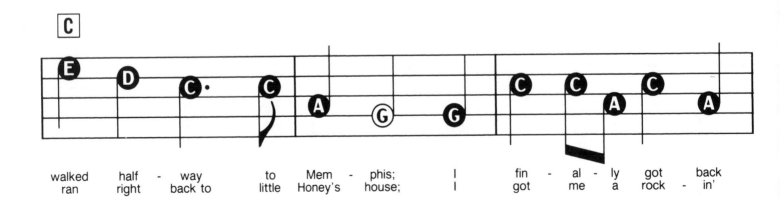

walked half - way to Mem - phis; I fin - al - ly got back
ran right back to little Honey's house; I got me a rock - in'

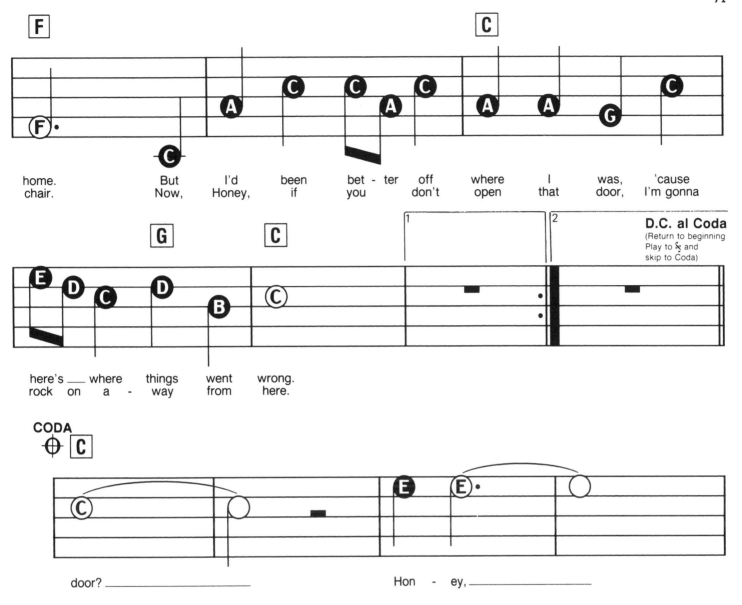

home.   But   I'd   been   bet - ter   off   where   I   was,   'cause
chair.   Now,   Honey,   if   you   don't   open   that   door,   I'm gonna

here's — where   things   went   wrong.
rock   on   a - way   from   here.

CODA

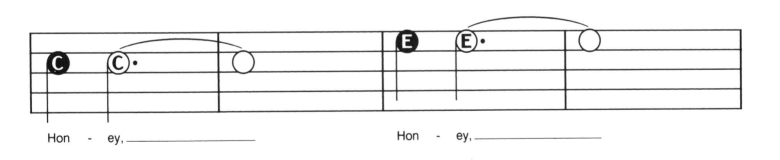

door? _____   Hon - ey, _____

Hon - ey, _____   Hon - ey, _____

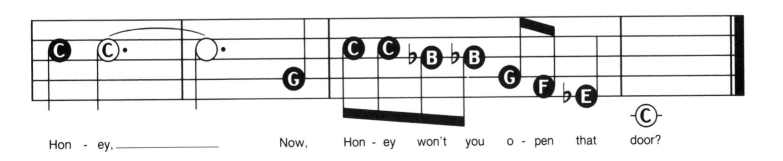

Hon - ey, _____   Now,   Hon - ey won't you o - pen that door?

Help Me Make It Through the Night

Registration 2
Rhythm: Rock or 8 Beat

Words and Music by
Kris Kristofferson

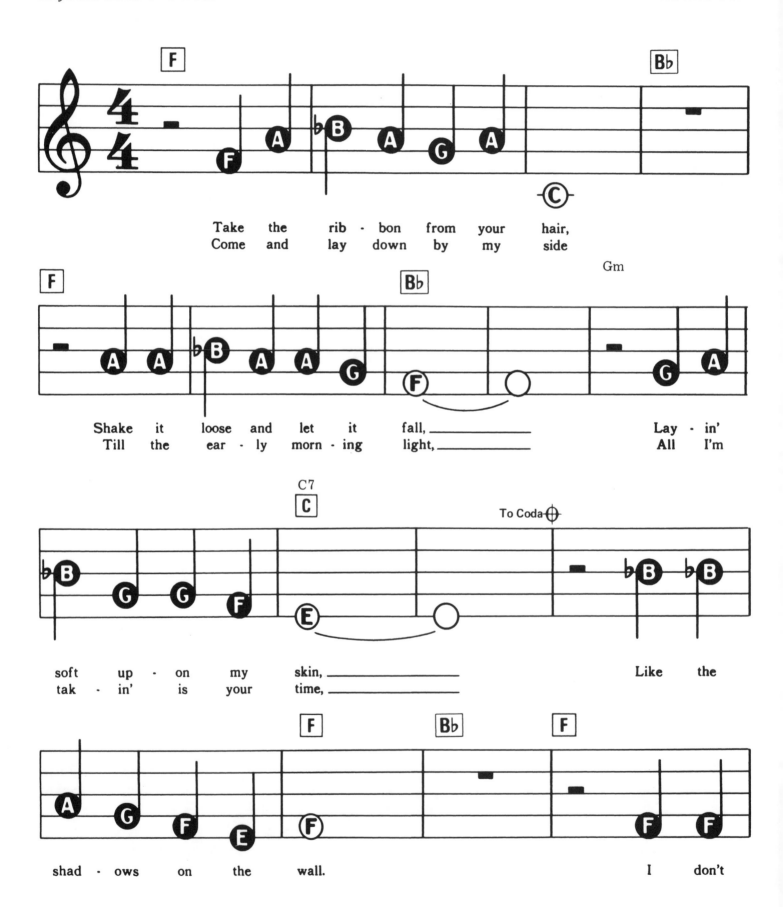

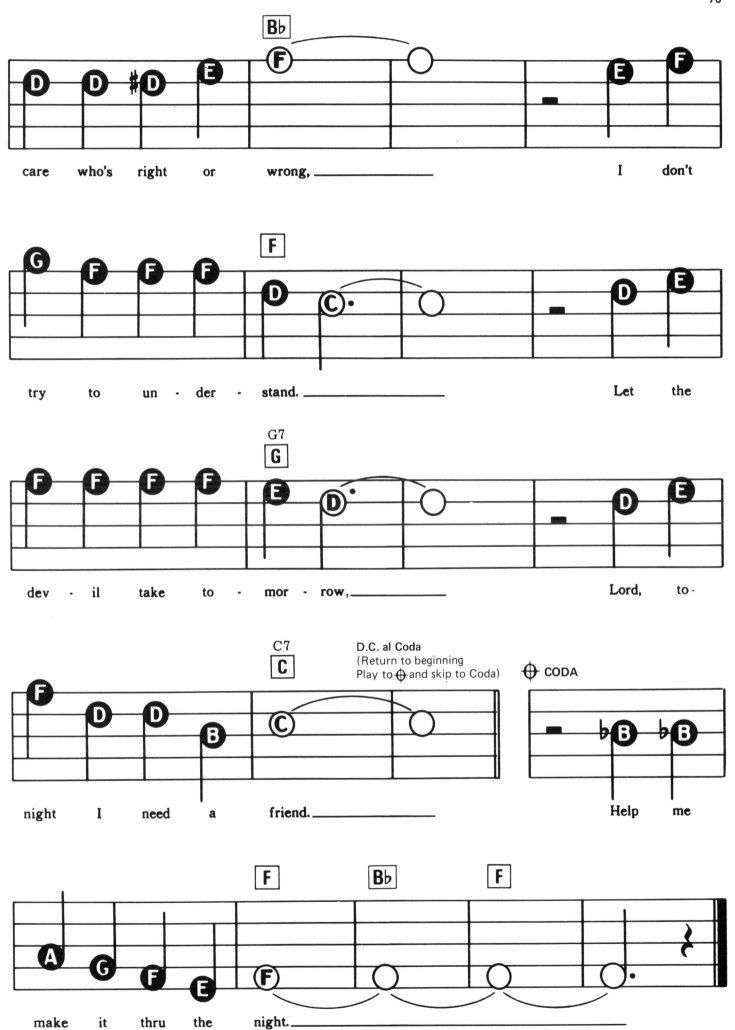

(I Never Promised You A)
Rose Garden

Registration 4
Rhythm: Fox Trot

Words and Music by
Joe South

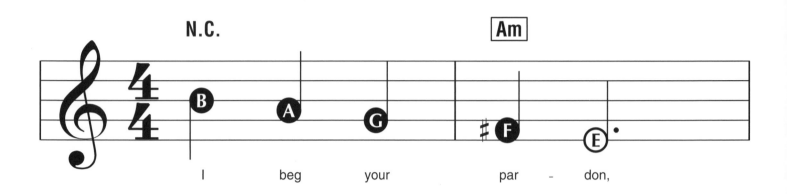

I beg your par - don,

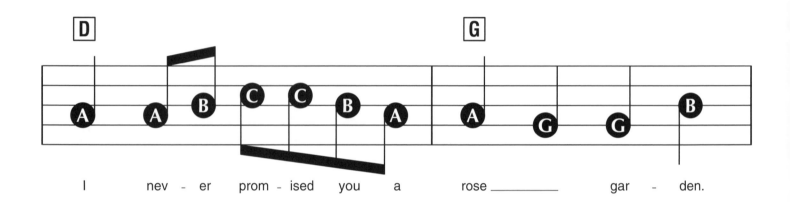

I nev - er prom - ised you a rose _____ gar - den.

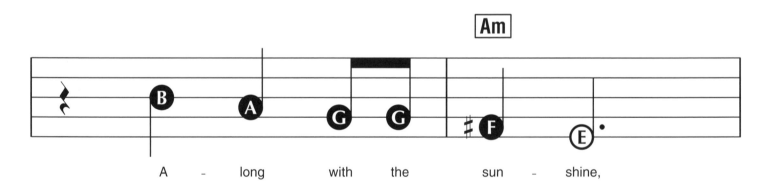

A - long with the sun - shine,

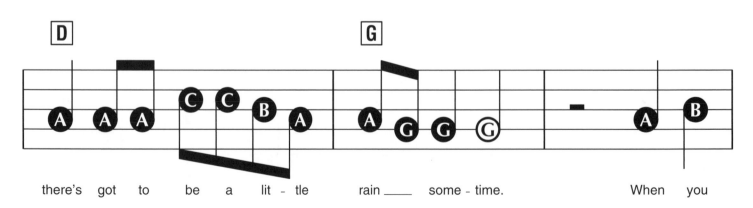

there's got to be a lit - tle rain ___ some - time.   When you

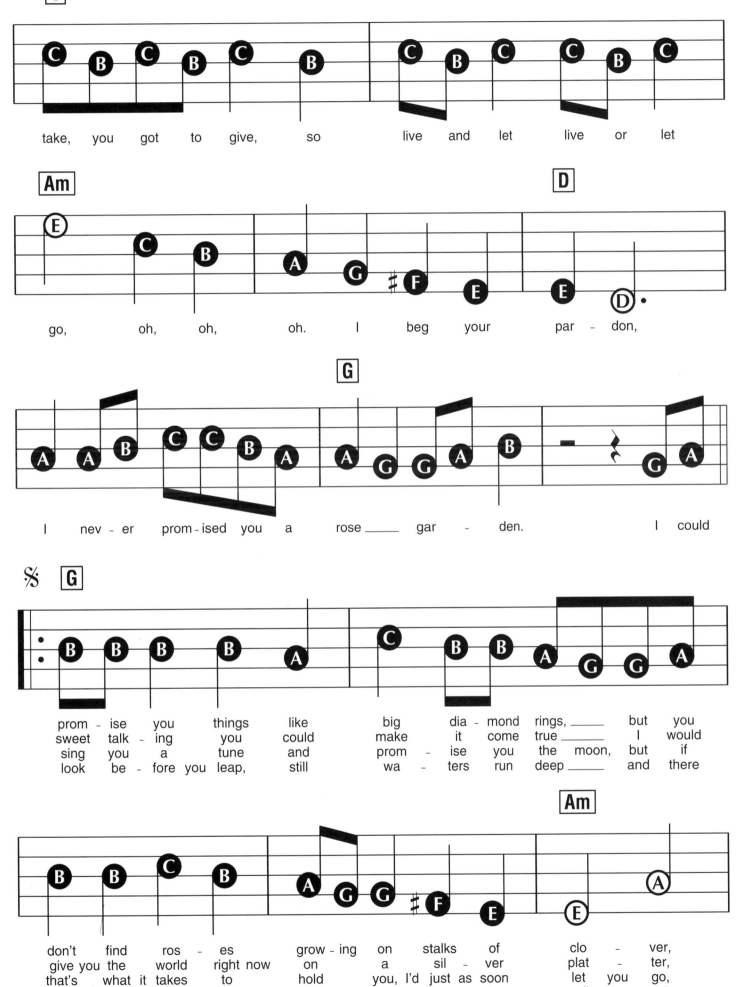

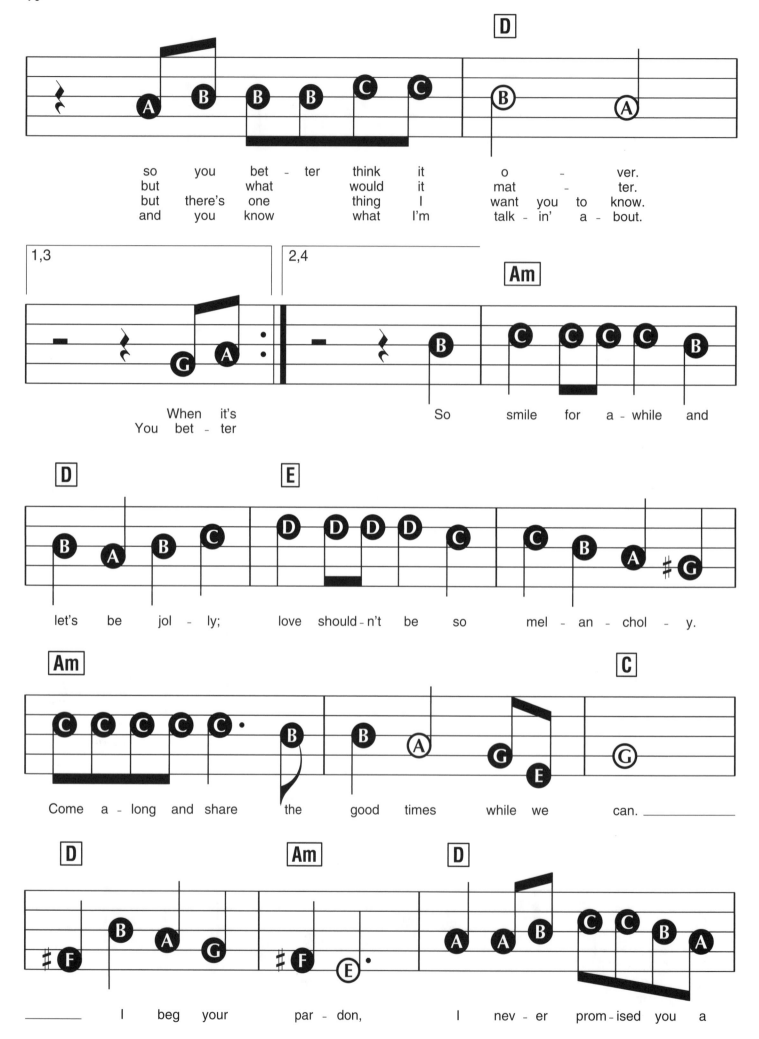

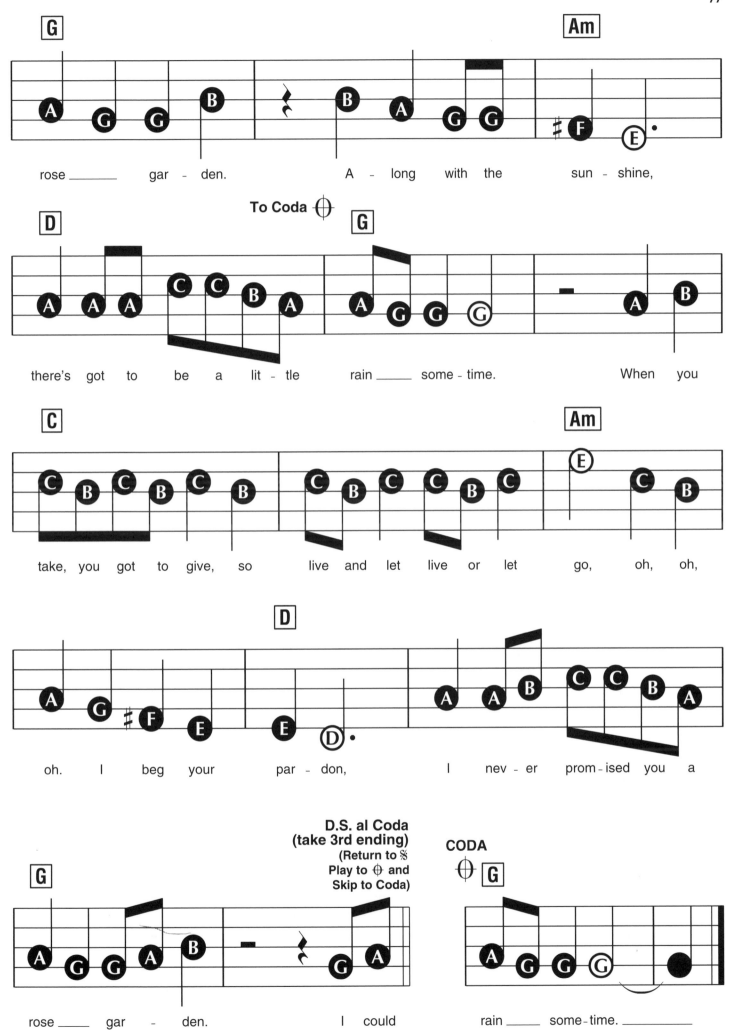

I'm Not Lisa

Registration 2
Rhythm: Country

Words and Music by
Jessi Colter

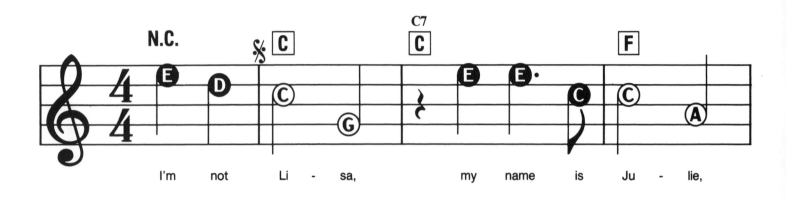

I'm not Li - sa, my name is Ju - lie,

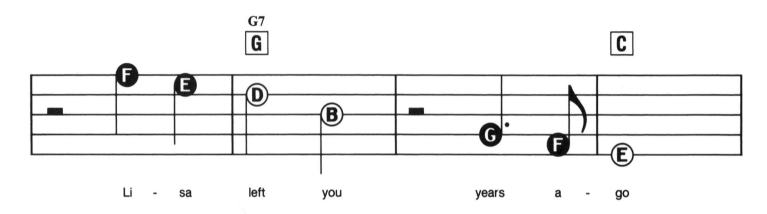

Li - sa left you years a - go

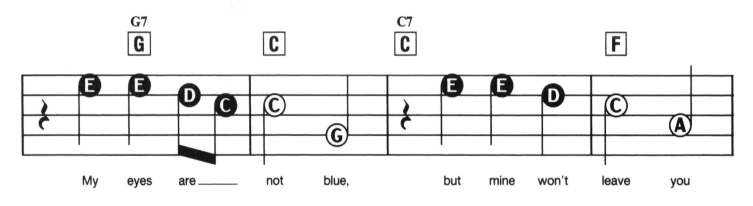

My eyes are _____ not blue, but mine won't leave you

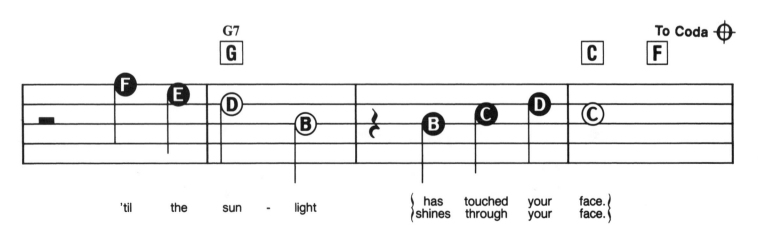

'til the sun - light {has touched your face.}
{shines through your face.}

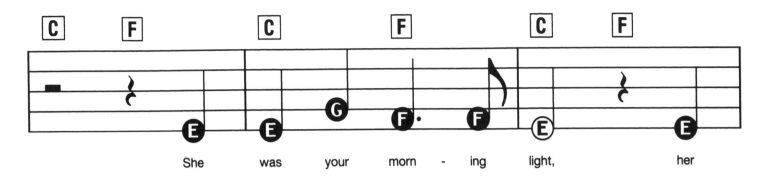

She was your morn - ing light, her

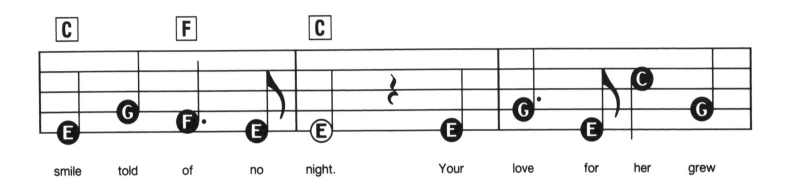

smile told of no night. Your love for her grew

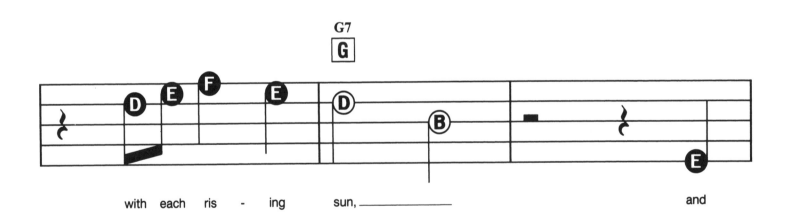

with each ris - ing sun, _____ and

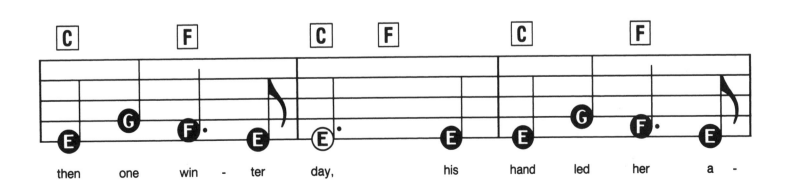

then one win - ter day, his hand led her a -

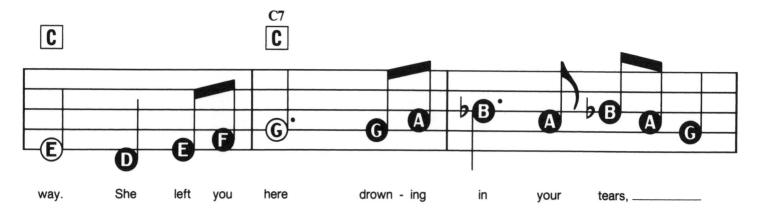

C | C7 C

way. She left you here drown - ing in your tears, _____

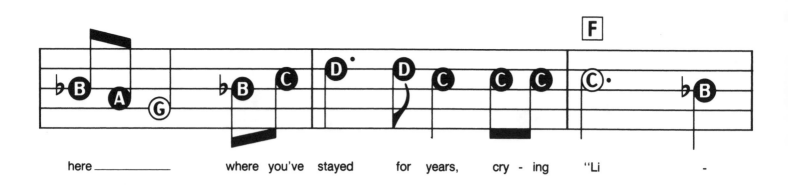

F

here _____ where you've stayed for years, cry - ing "Li -

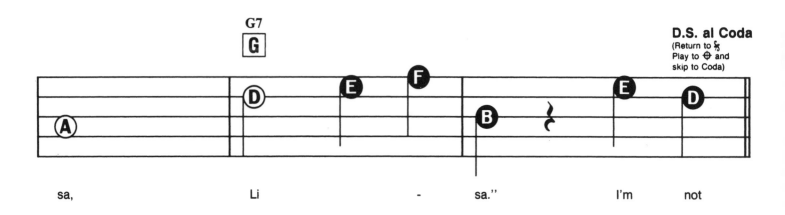

G7 G

D.S. al Coda
(Return to 𝄋
Play to ⊕ and
skip to Coda)

sa, Li - sa." I'm not

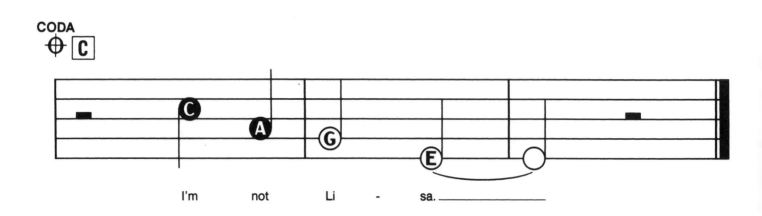

CODA
⊕ C

I'm not Li - sa. _____

I've Got a Tiger by the Tail

Registration 9
Rhythm: Country or Fox Trot

Words and Music by Buck Owens
and Harlan Howard

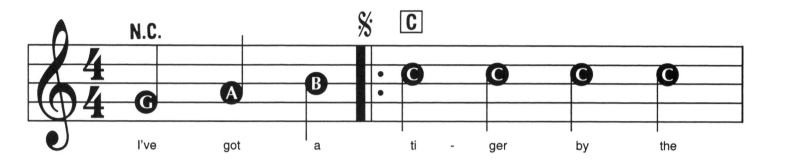

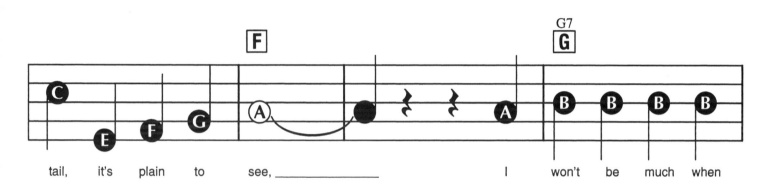

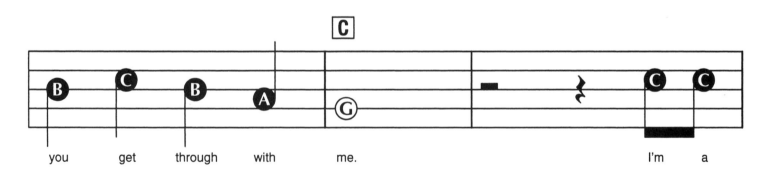

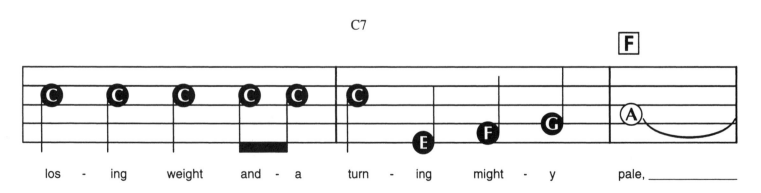

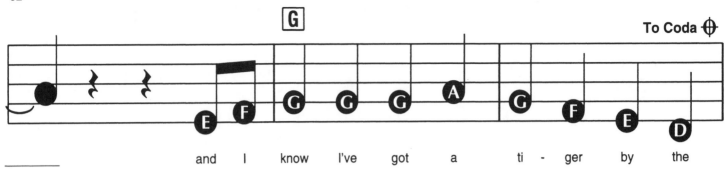

and I know I've got a ti - ger by the

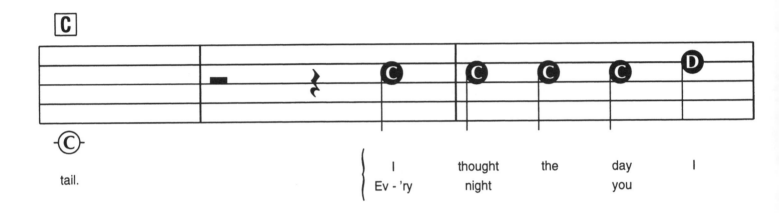

tail.
I thought the day I
Ev - 'ry night you

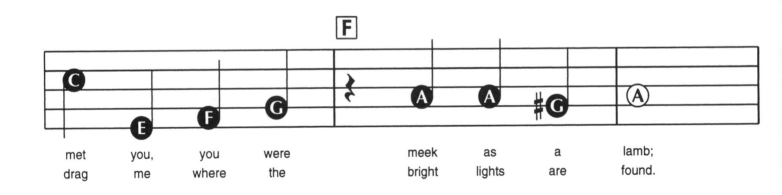

met you, you were the meek as a lamb;
drag me where you were bright lights are found.

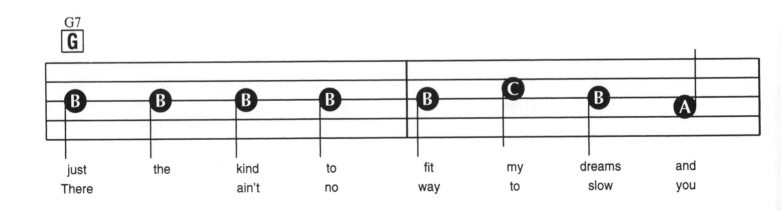

just the kind to fit my dreams and
There ain't no way to slow you

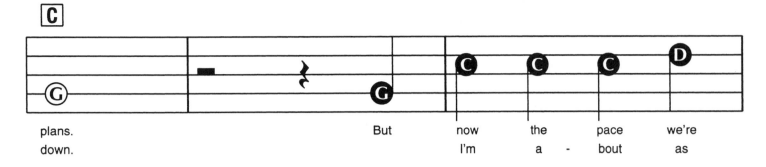

plans.
down.

But now the pace we're
I'm a - bout as

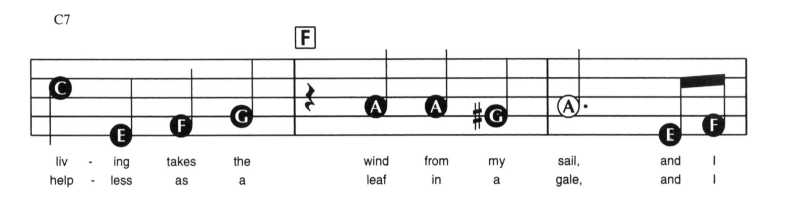

C7

liv - ing takes the wind from my sail, and I
help - less as a leaf in a gale, and I

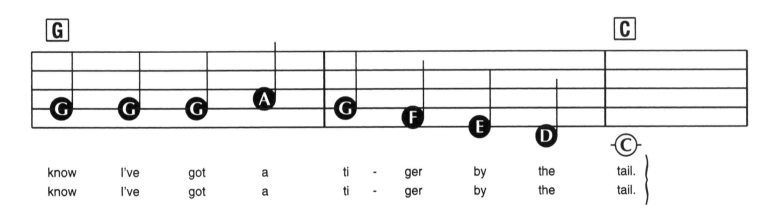

know I've got a ti - ger by the tail.
know I've got a ti - ger by the tail.

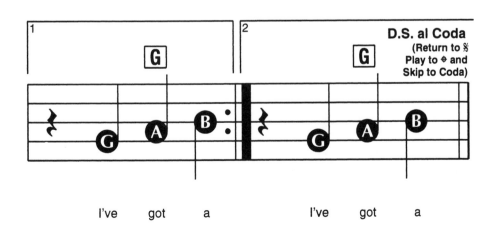

D.S. al Coda
(Return to ℅
Play to ⊕ and
Skip to Coda)

I've got a
I've got a

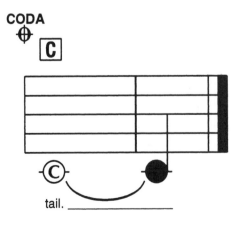

CODA

tail. _____

In the Jailhouse Now

Registration 8
Rhythm: Country Swing or Fox Trot

Words and Music by
Jimmie Rodgers

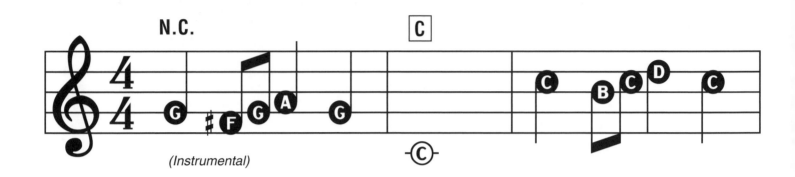

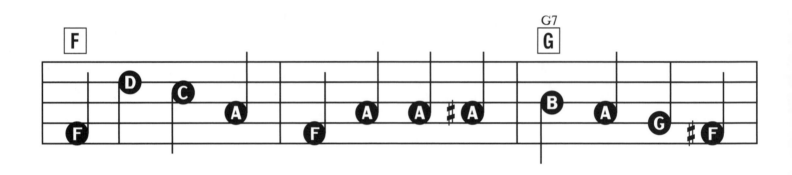

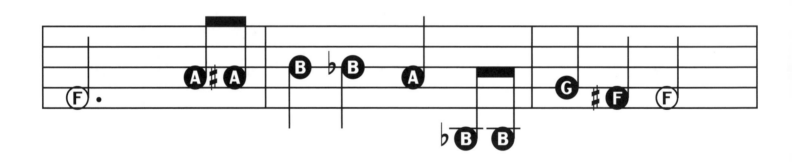

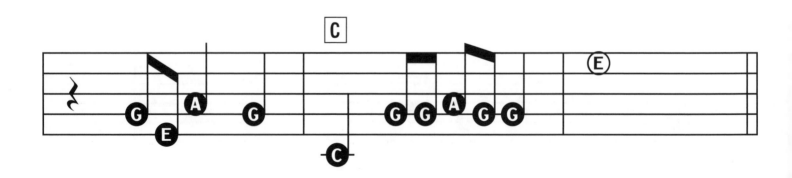

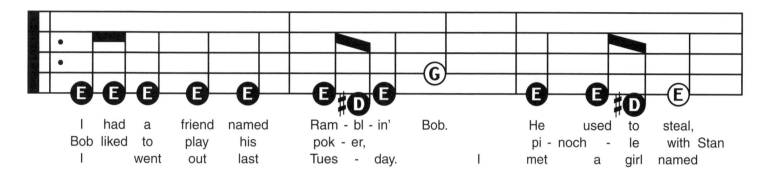

I had a friend named Ram - bl - in' Bob. He used to steal,
Bob liked to play his pok - er, pi - noch - le with Stan
I went out last Tues - day. I met a girl named

C7

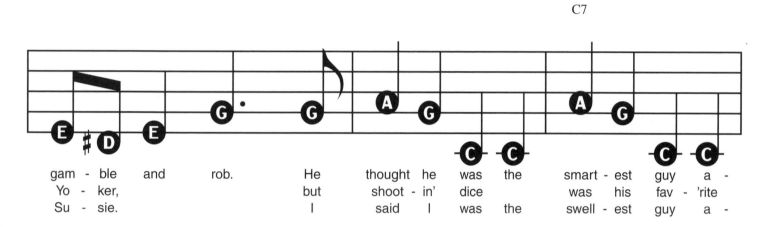

gam - ble and rob. He thought he was the smart - est guy a -
Yo - ker, but shoot - in' dice was his fav - 'rite
Su - sie. I said I was the swell - est guy a -

F

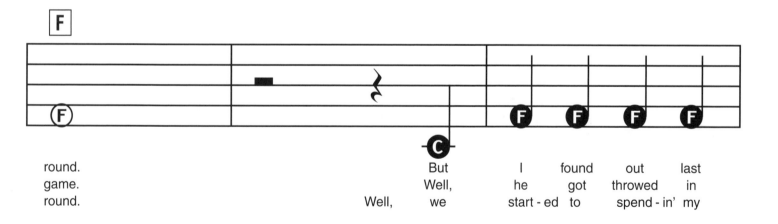

round. But I found out last
game. Well, he got throwed in
round. Well, we start - ed to spend - in' my

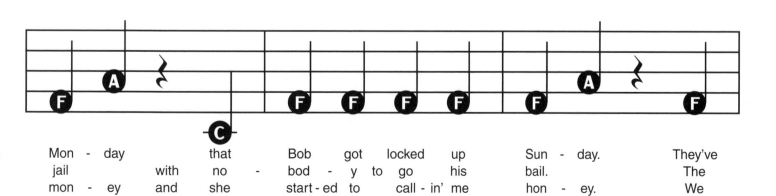

Mon - day that Bob got locked up Sun - day. They've
jail with no - bod - y to go his bail. The
mon - ey and she start - ed to call - in' me hon - ey. We

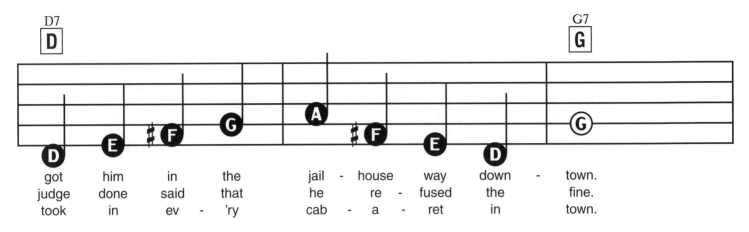

got him in the jail - house way down - town.
judge done said that he re - fused the fine.
took in ev - 'ry cab - a - ret in town.

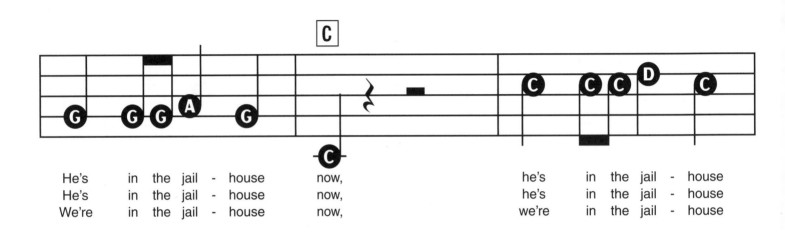

He's in the jail - house now, he's in the jail - house
He's in the jail - house now, he's in the jail - house
We're in the jail - house now, we're in the jail - house

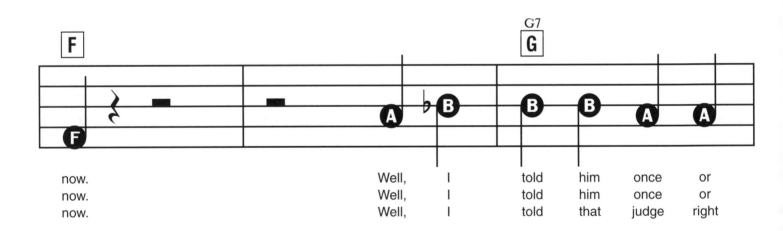

now. Well, I told him once or
now. Well, I told him once or
now. Well, I told that judge right

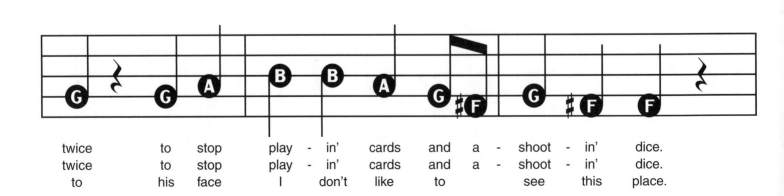

twice to stop play - in' cards and a - shoot - in' dice.
twice to stop play - in' cards and a - shoot - in' dice.
to his face I don't like to see this place.

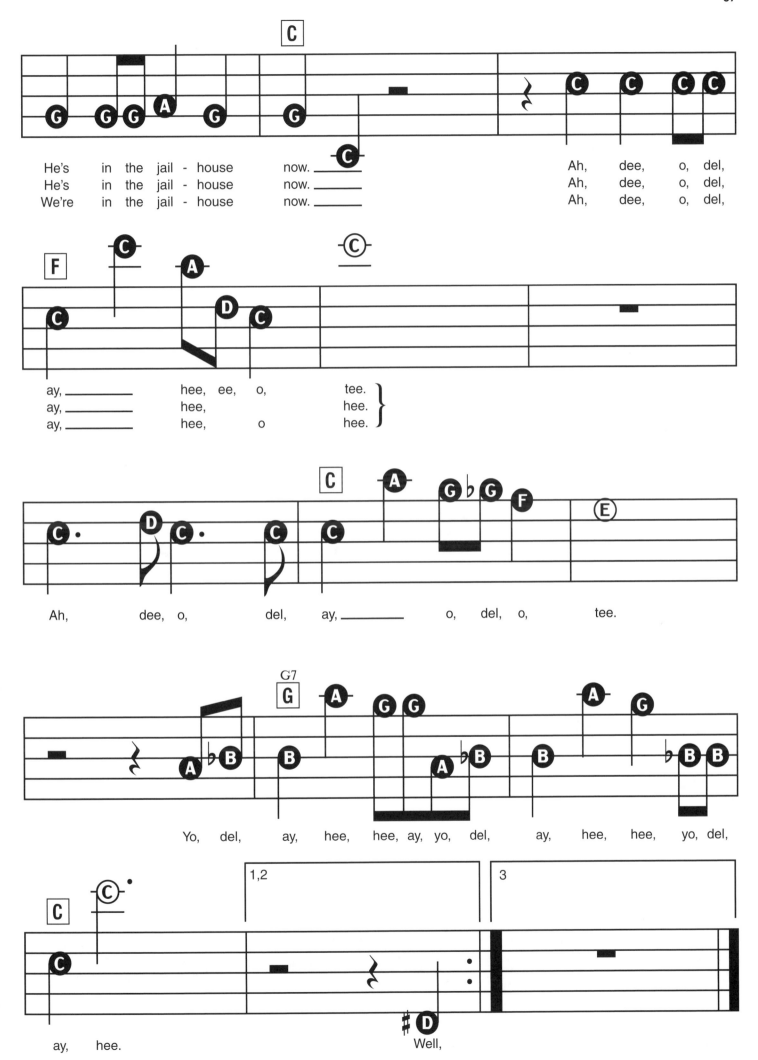

I.O.U.

Registration 10
Rhythm: Ballad or Rock

Words and Music by Kerry Chater
and Austin Roberts

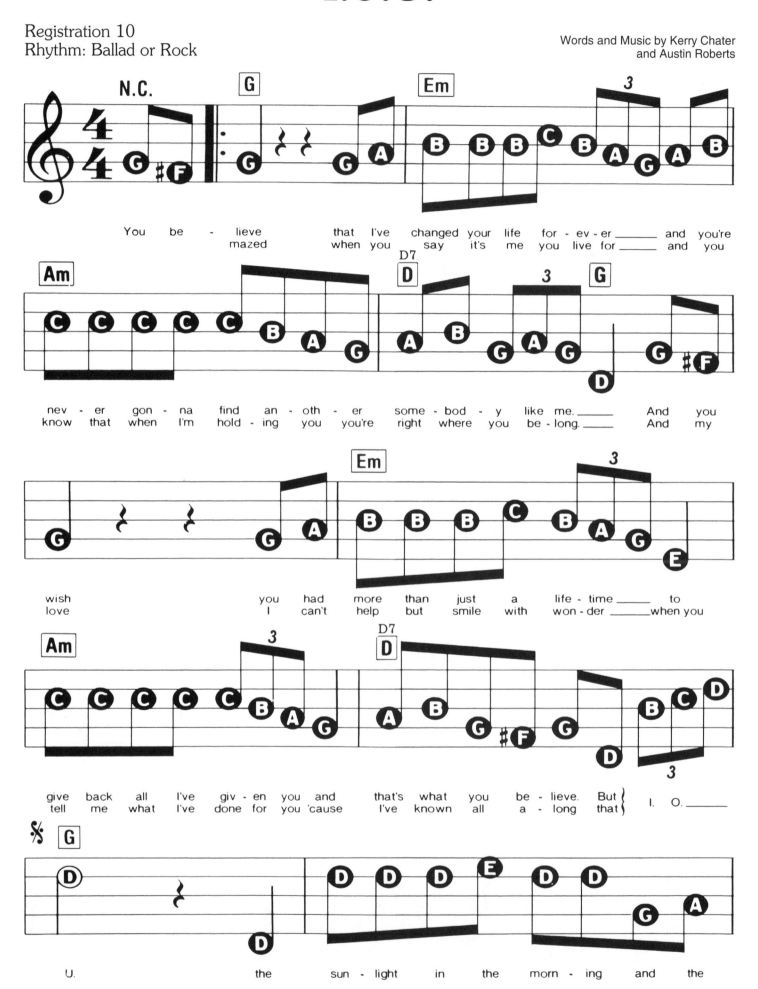

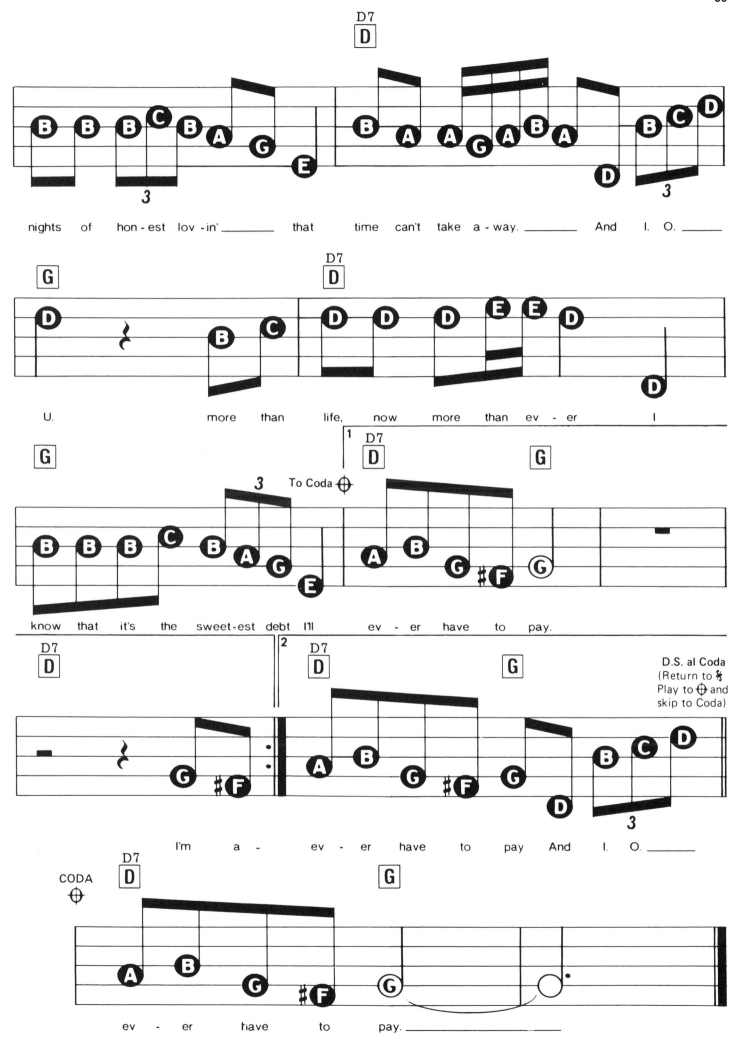

The Last Cheater's Waltz

Registration 2
Rhythm: Waltz

Words and Music by
Sonny Throckmorton

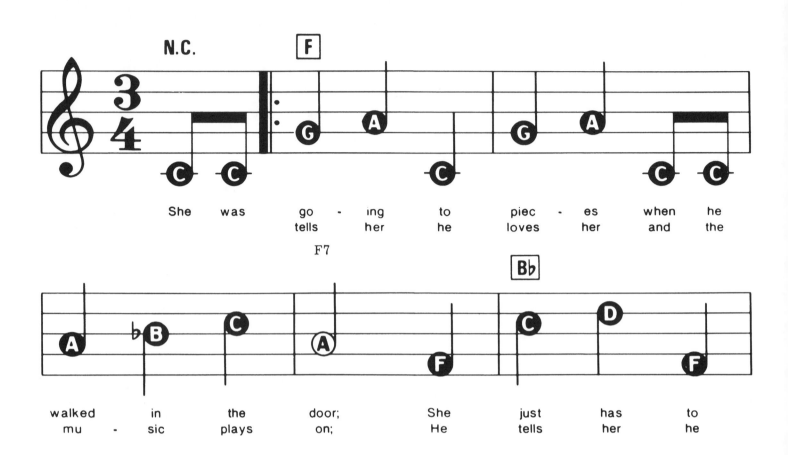

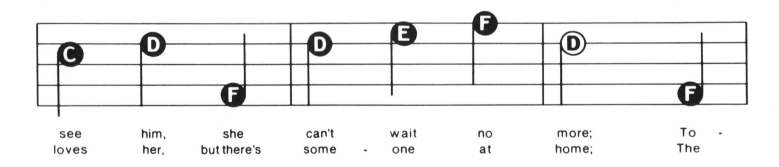

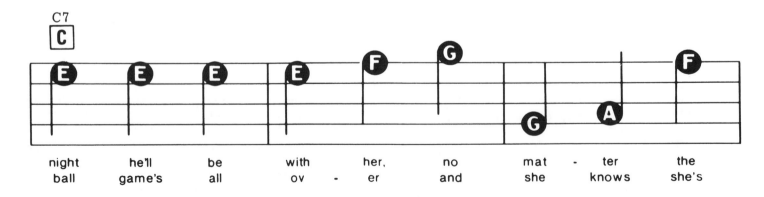

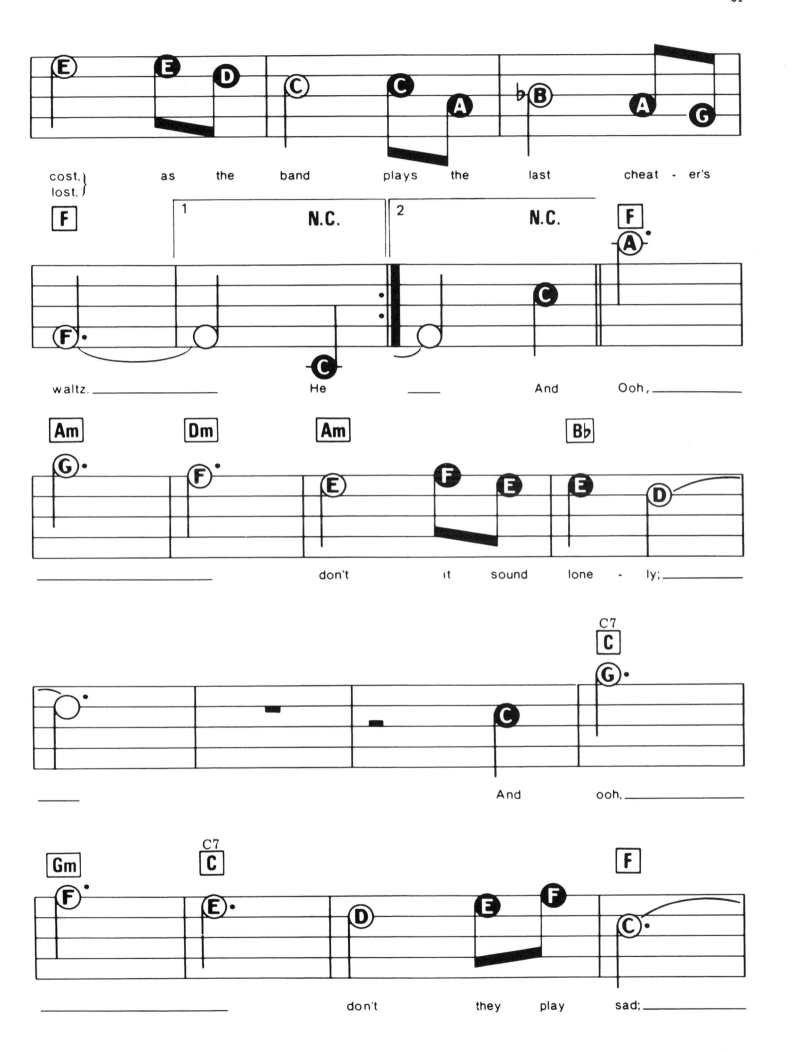

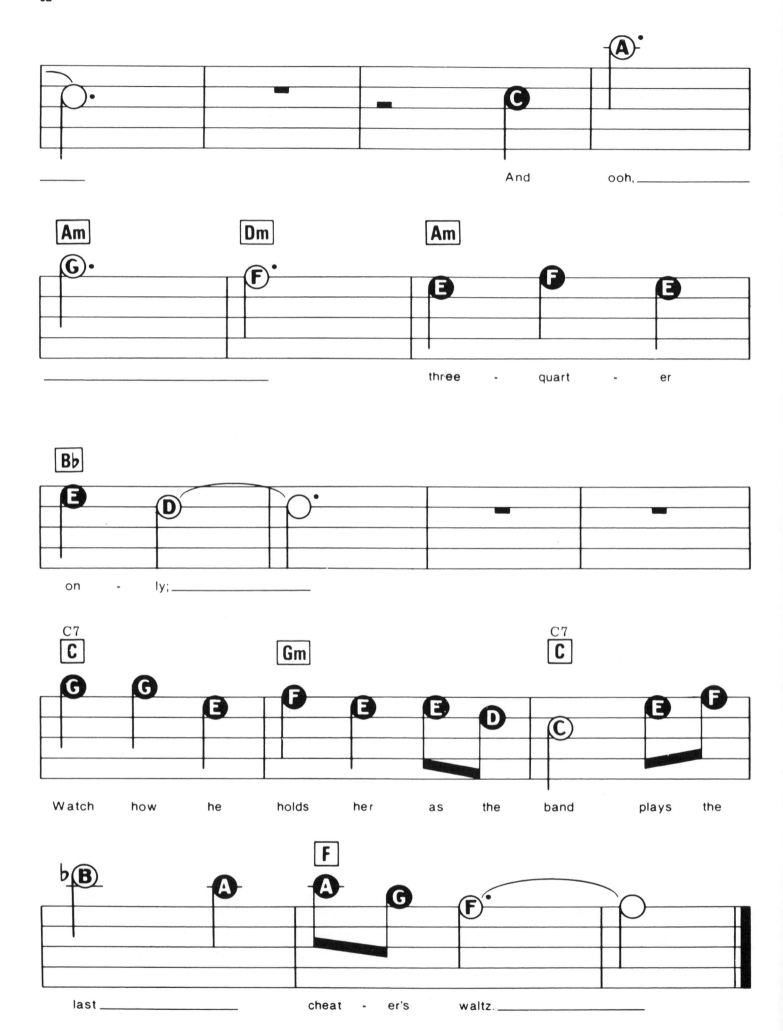

Lucille

Registration 2
Rhythm: Waltz

Words and Music by Roger Bowling
and Hal Bynum

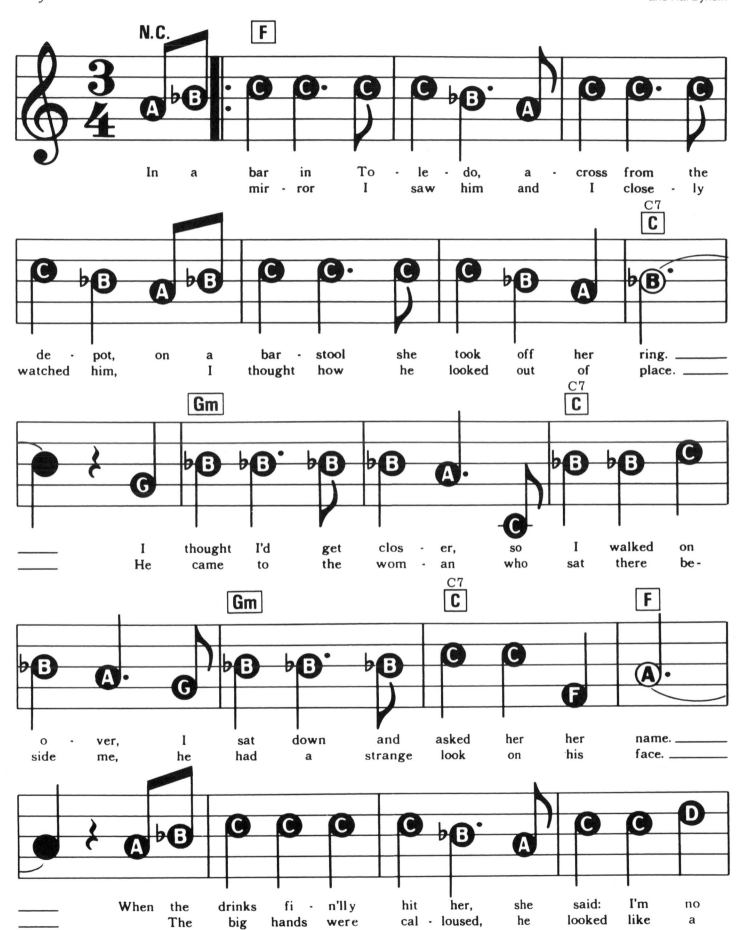

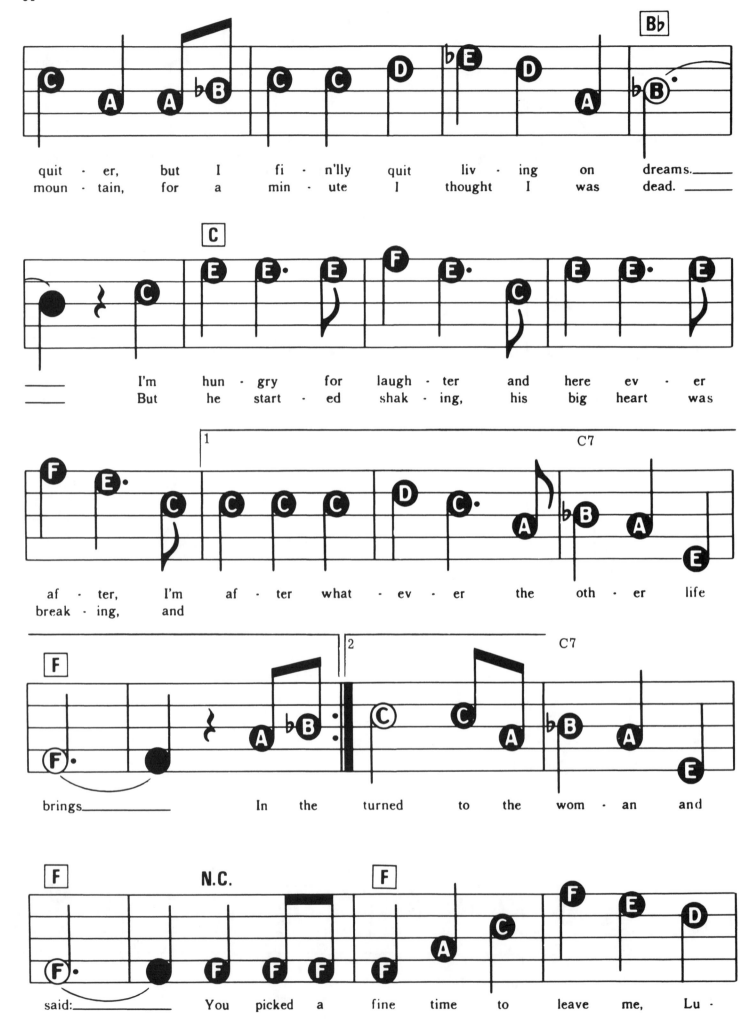

quit - er, but I fi - n'lly quit liv - ing on dreams._____
moun - tain, for a min - ute I thought I was dead. _____

_____ I'm hun - gry for laugh - ter and here ev - er
_____ But he start - ed shak - ing, and his big heart was

af - ter, I'm af - ter what - ev - er the oth - er life
break - ing, and

brings_____ In the turned to the wom - an and

said:_____ You picked a fine time to leave me, Lu -

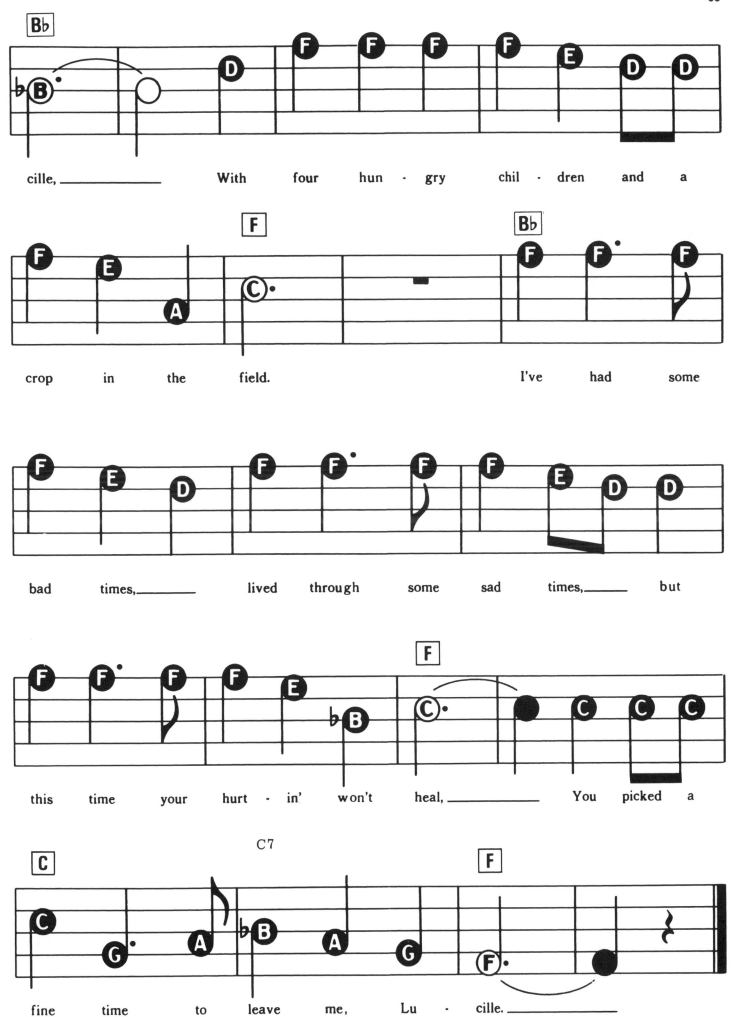

Mammas Don't Let Your Babies Grow Up to Be Cowboys

Registration 2
Rhythm: Waltz

Words and Music by Ed Bruce
and Patsy Bruce

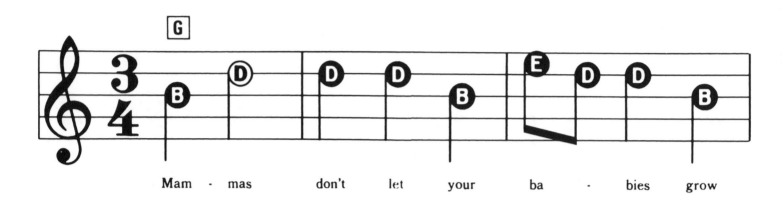

Mam - mas don't let your ba - bies grow

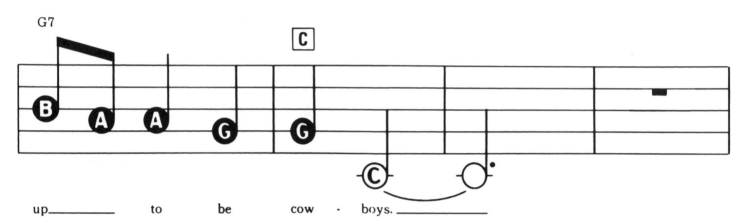

up_____ to be cow - boys. _____

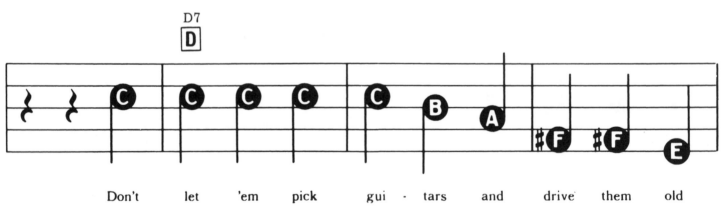

Don't let 'em pick gui - tars and drive them old

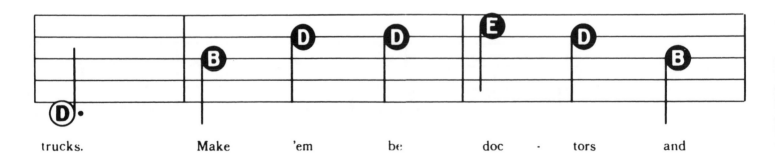

trucks. Make 'em be doc - tors and

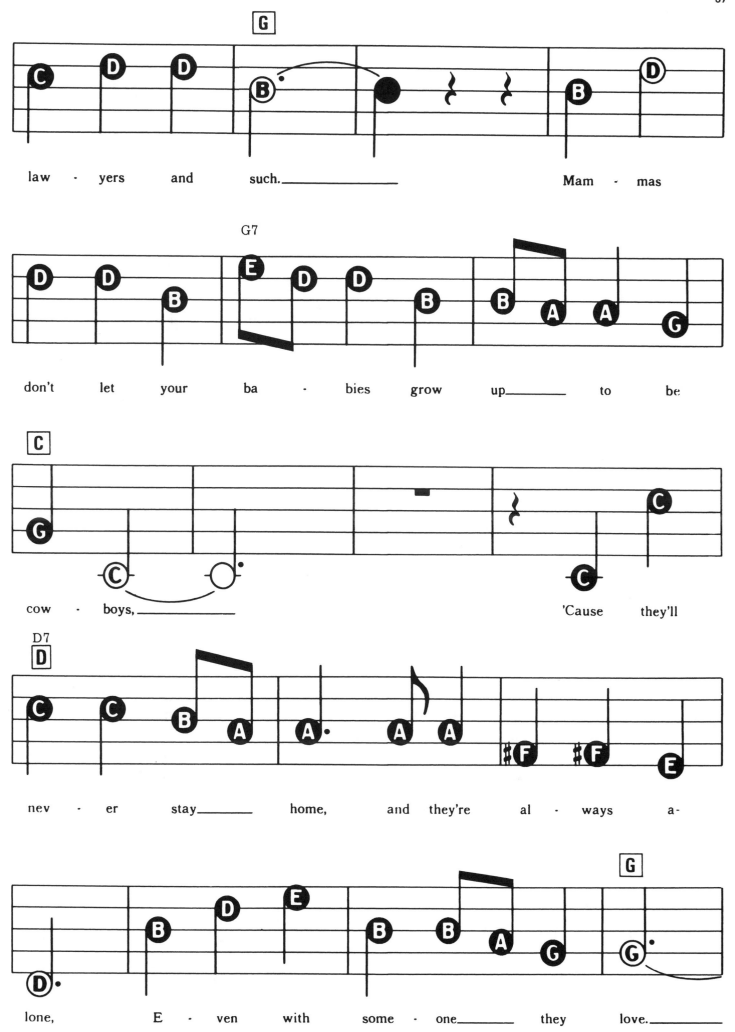

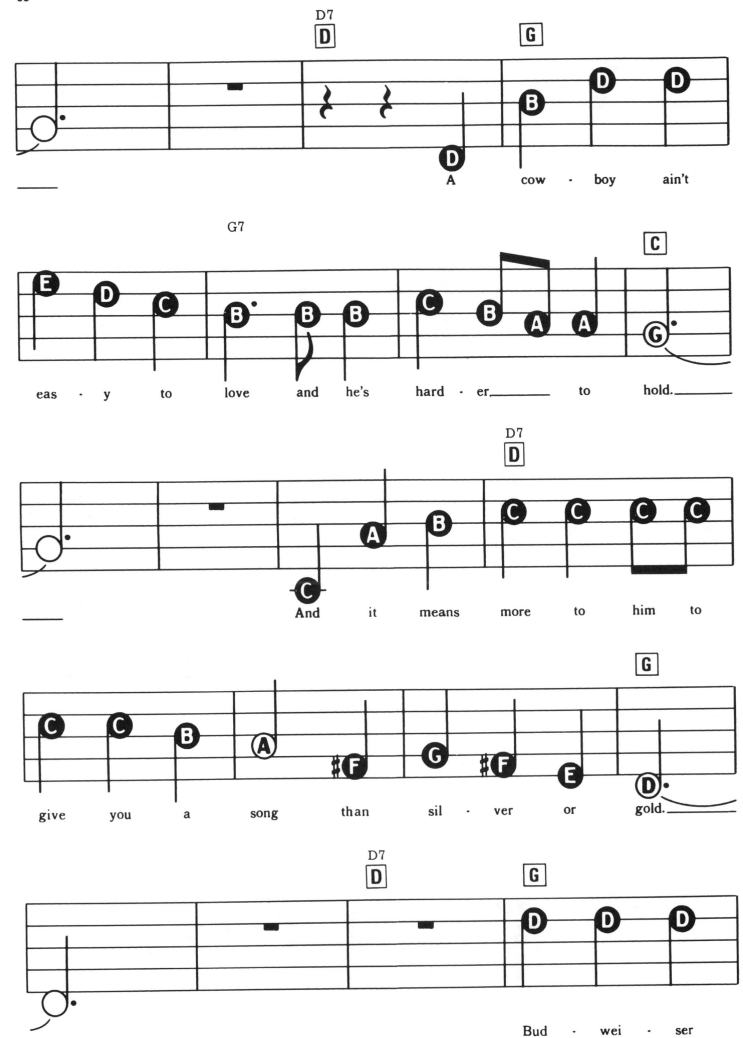

G7

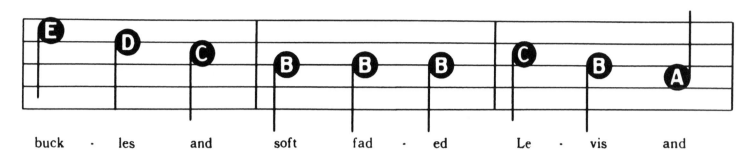

buck · les and soft fad · ed Le · vis and

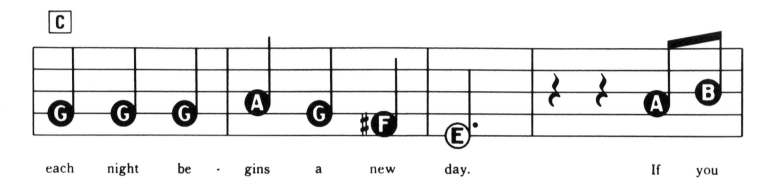

each night be · gins a new day. If you

D7

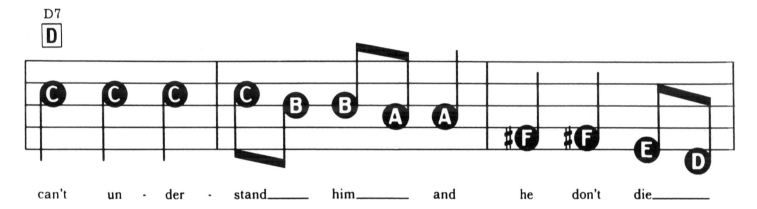

can't un · der · stand____ him____ and he don't die____

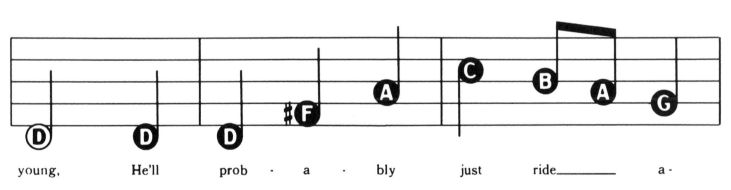

young, He'll prob · a · bly just ride____ a-

D7

D.C. and Fade
(Return to beginning
and Fade)

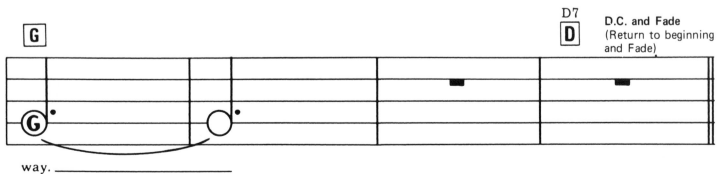

way. _____

My Heroes Have Always Been Cowboys

Registration 9
Rhythm: Waltz

Words and Music by
Sharon Vaughn

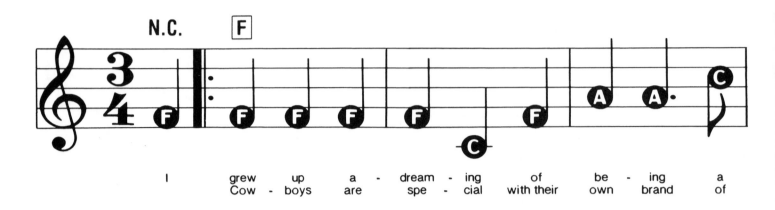

I grew up a - dream - ing of be - ing a
Cow - boys are spe - cial with their own brand of

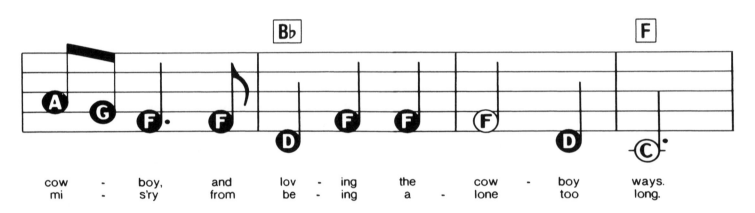

cow - boy, and lov - ing the cow - boy ways.
mi - s'ry from be - ing a - lone too long.

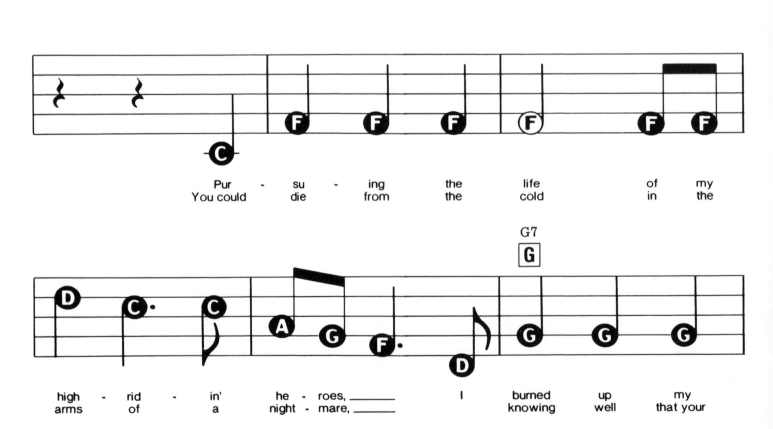

Pur - su - ing the life of my
You could die from the cold in the

high - rid - in' he - roes, _____ I burned up my
arms of a night - mare, _____ knowing well that your

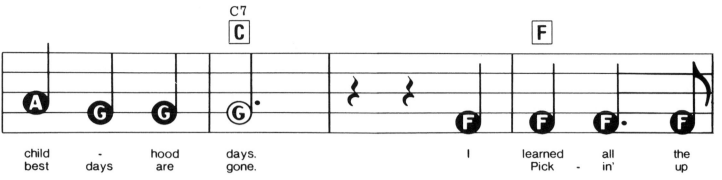

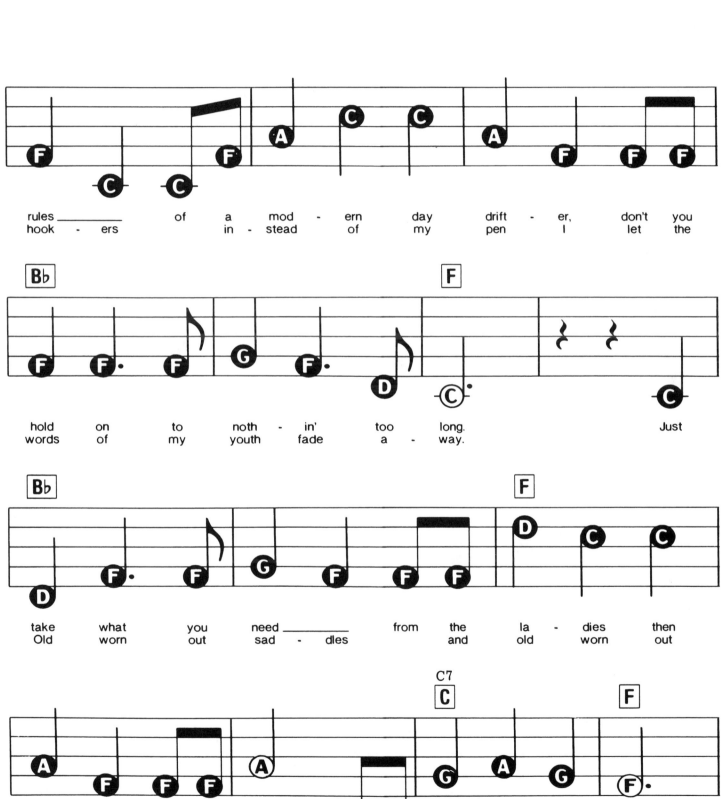

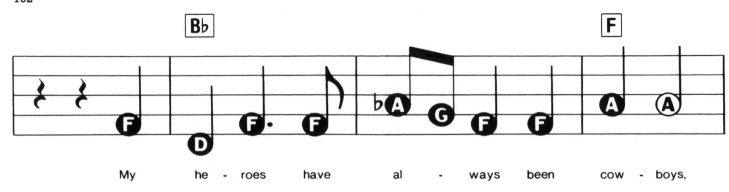

My he - roes have al - ways been cow - boys,

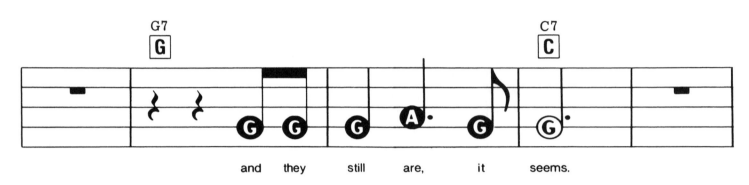

and they still are, it seems.

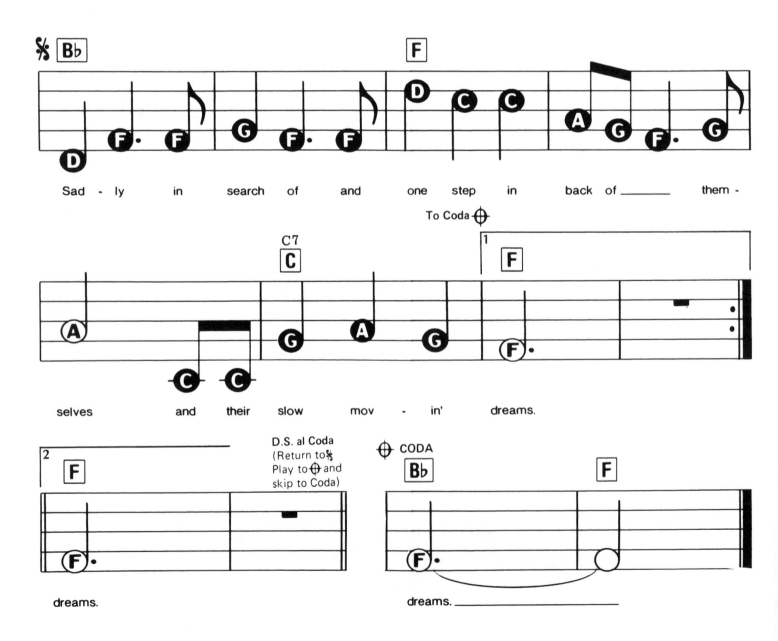

Sad - ly in search of and one step in back of _____ them -

To Coda ⊕

selves and their slow mov - in' dreams.

D.S. al Coda
(Return to %
Play to ⊕ and
skip to Coda)

⊕ CODA

dreams.

dreams. _____

Shadows in the Moonlight

Registration 2
Rhythm: Rock or 8-Beat

Words and Music by Charlie Black
and Rory Bourke

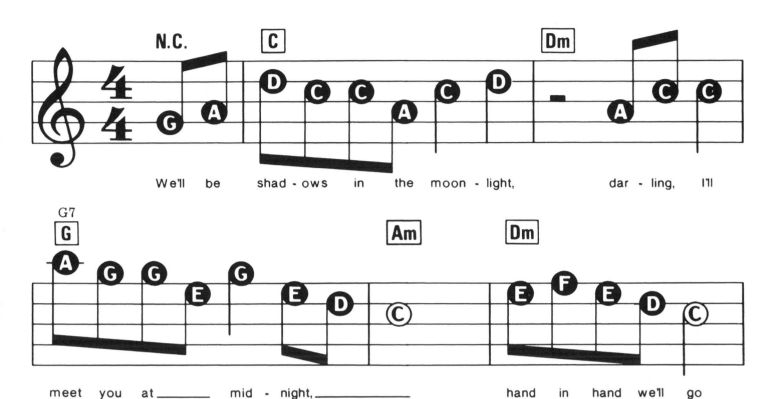

We'll be shad - ows in the moon - light, dar - ling, I'll

meet you at _____ mid - night, _____ hand in hand we'll go

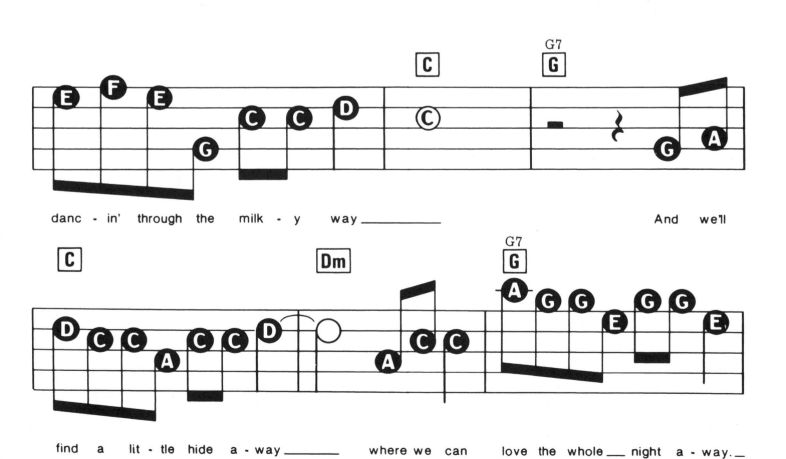

danc - in' through the milk - y way _____ And we'll

find a lit - tle hide a - way _____ where we can love the whole ___ night a - way. ___

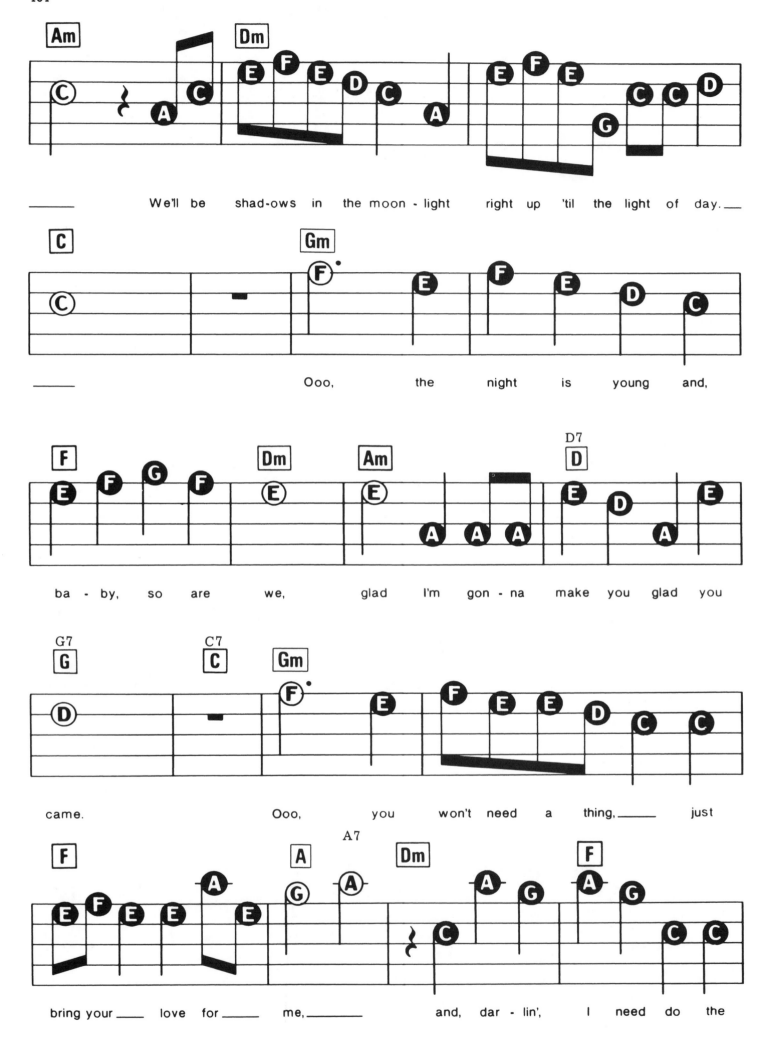

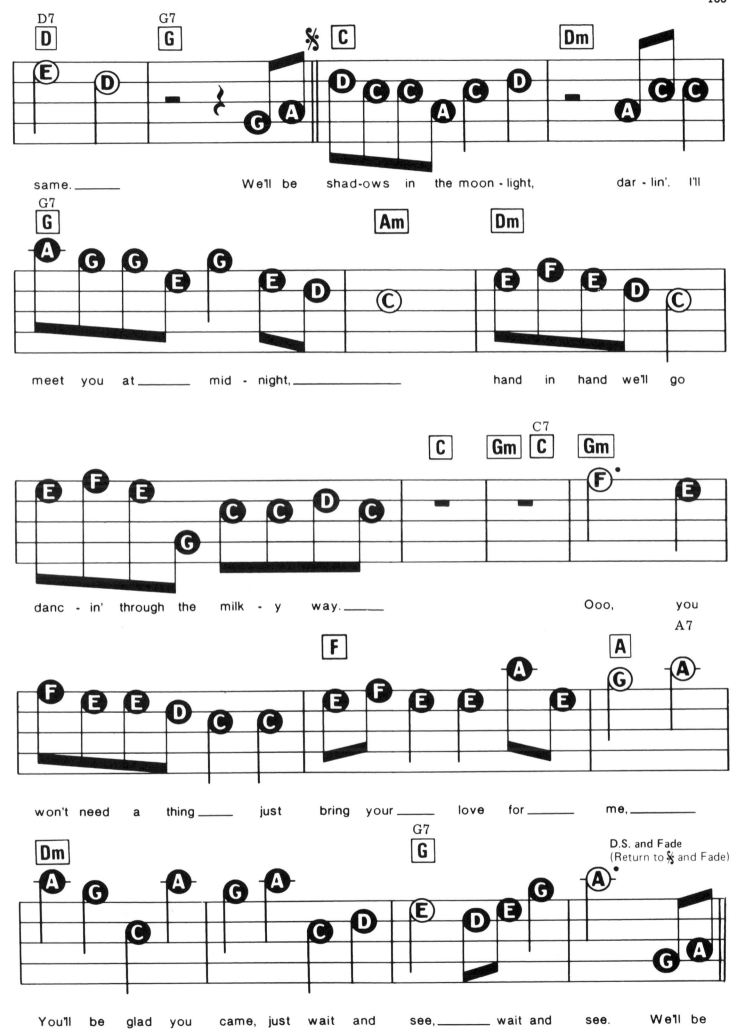

105

A Rainy Night in Georgia

Registration 5
Rhythm: Ballad or Fox Trot

Words and Music by
Tony Joe White

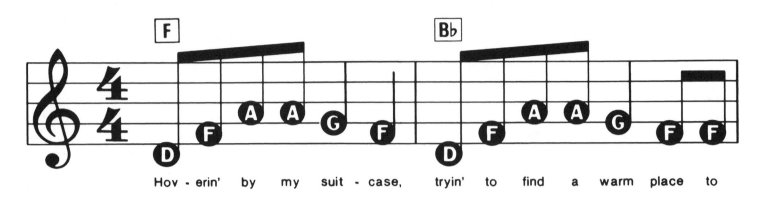

Hov - erin' by my suit - case, tryin' to find a warm place to

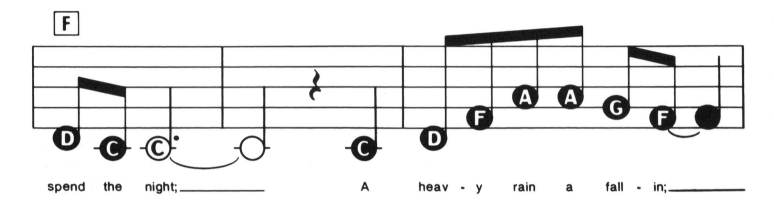

spend the night;_____ A heav - y rain a fall - in;_____

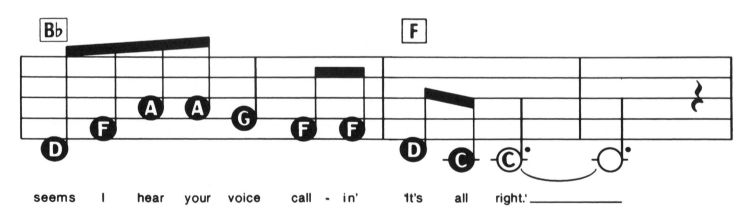

seems I hear your voice call - in' 'It's all right.'_____

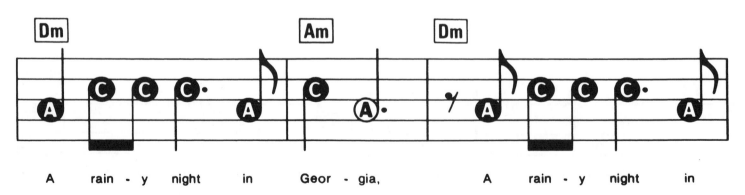

A rain - y night in Geor - gia, A rain - y night in

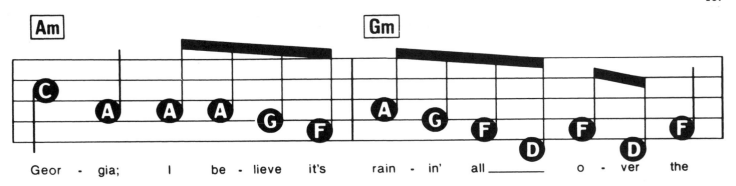

Geor - gia; I be - lieve it's rain - in' all _____ o - ver the

world. _____

How man - y times I've won - dered; It still comes out the

same; No mat - ter how you look at it, think of it; You

just got to do _____ your own thing. _____

D.C. al Fine
(Return to beginning
and play to Fine.)

Running Bear

Registration 9
Rhythm: Rock or 8 Beat

Words and Music by
J.P. Richardson

109

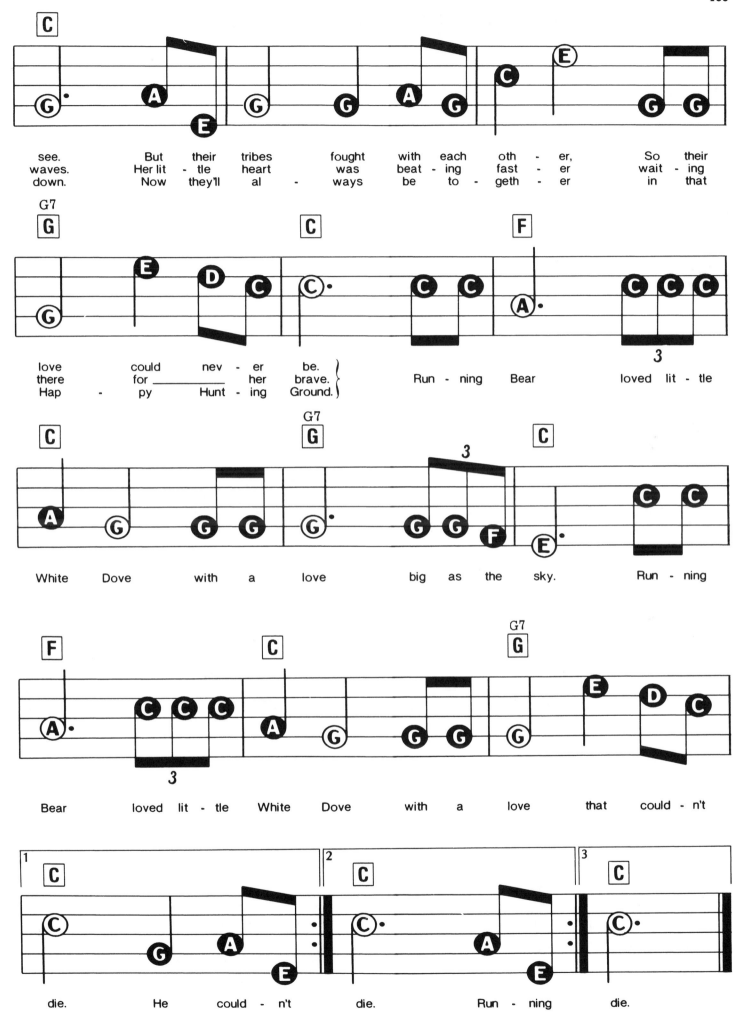

Sleeping Single in a Double Bed

Registration 1
Rhythm: Country

Words and Music by Dennis Morgan
and Kye Fleming

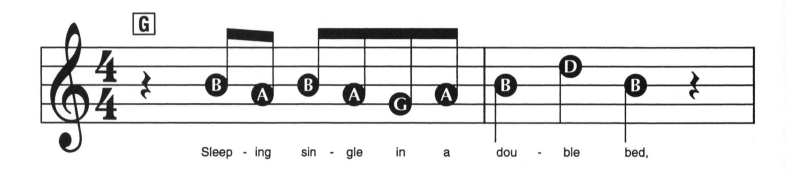

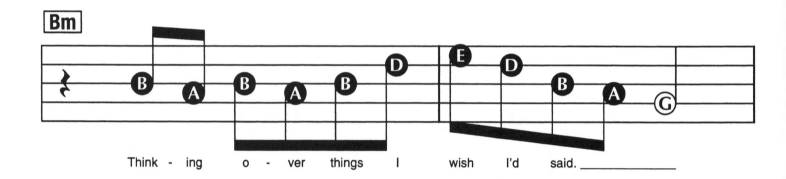

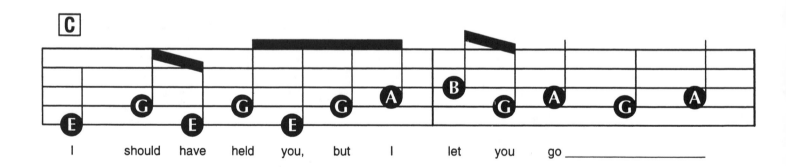

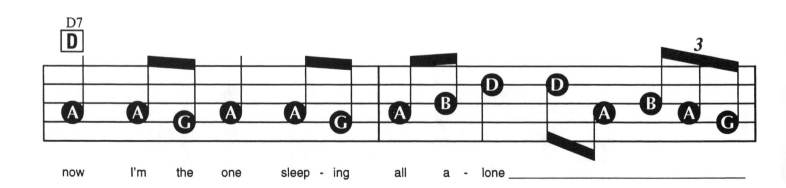

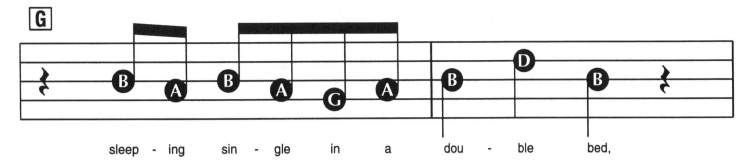

sleep - ing sin - gle in a dou - ble bed,

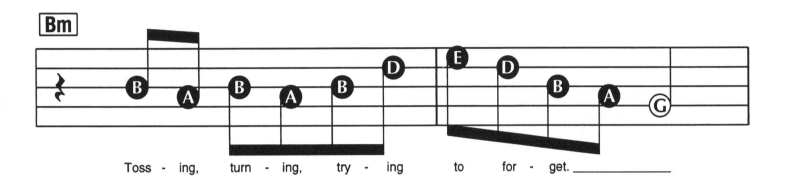

Toss - ing, turn - ing, try - ing to for - get. _____

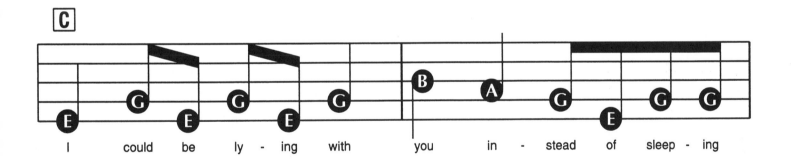

I could be ly - ing with you in - stead of sleep - ing

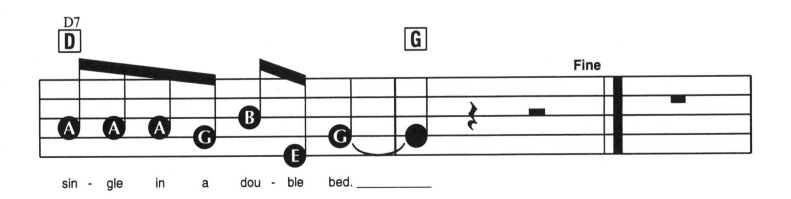

sin - gle in a dou - ble bed. _____

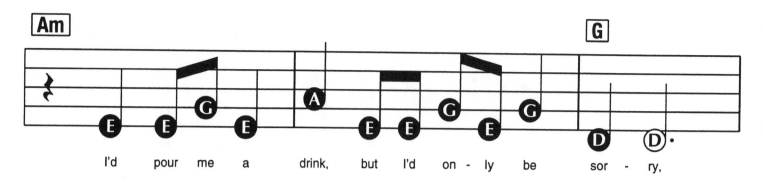

I'd   pour   me   a   drink,   but   I'd   on - ly   be   sor - ry,

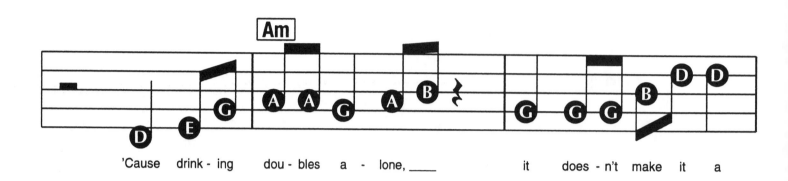

'Cause   drink - ing   dou - bles   a - lone, _____   it   does - n't   make   it   a

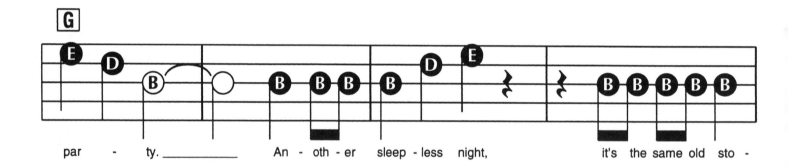

par - ty. _____   An - oth - er   sleep - less   night,   it's   the   same   old   sto -

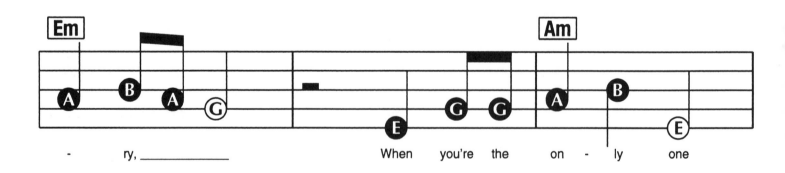

- ry, _____   When   you're   the   on - ly   one

D.C. al Fine
(Return to beginning
Play to Fine)

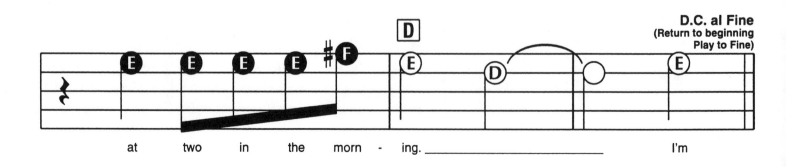

at   two   in   the   morn - ing. _____   I'm

Why Not Me

Registration 1
Rhythm: Country or Swing

Words and Music by Harlan Howard,
Sonny Throckmorton and Brent Maher

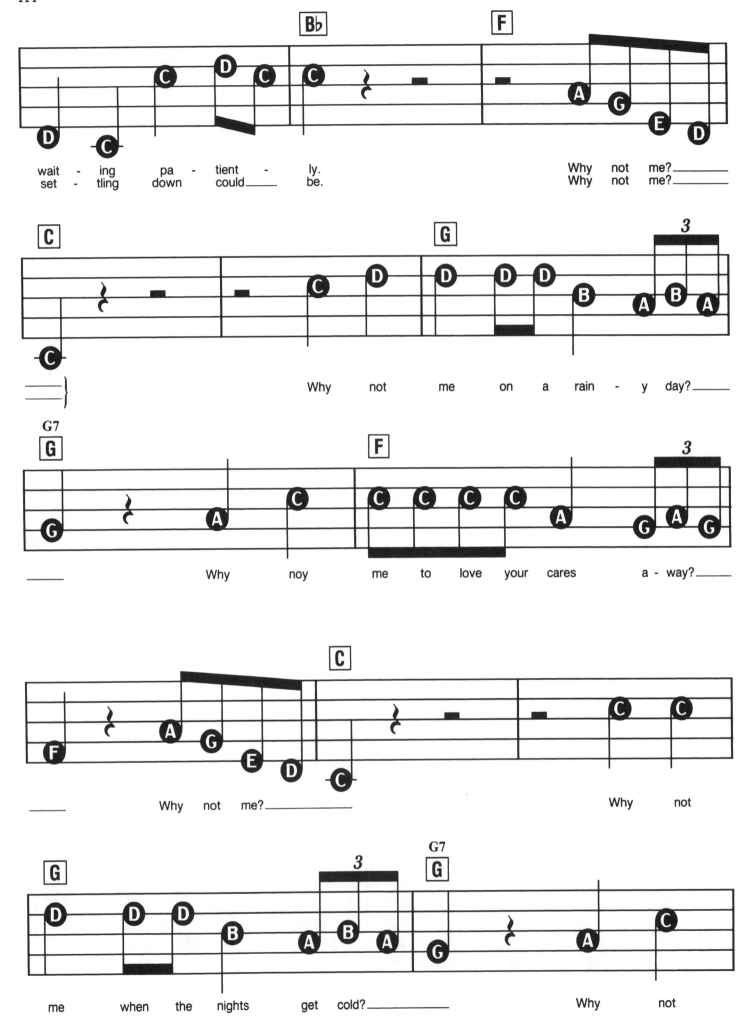

115

Up Against the Wall Redneck

Registration 3
Rhythm: Swing or Fox Trot

Words and Music by
Ray Wylie Hubbard

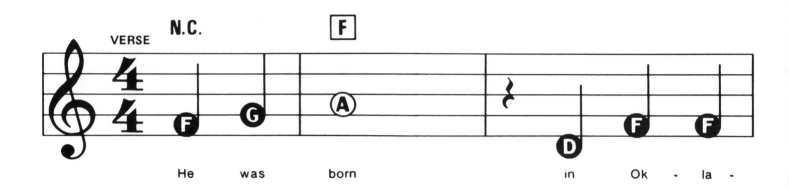

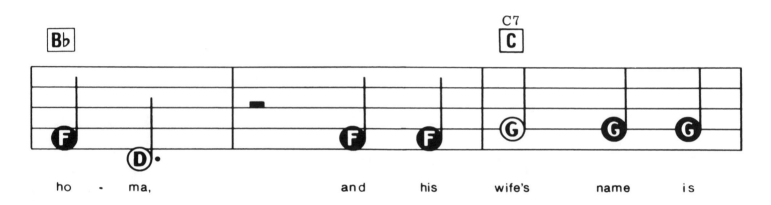

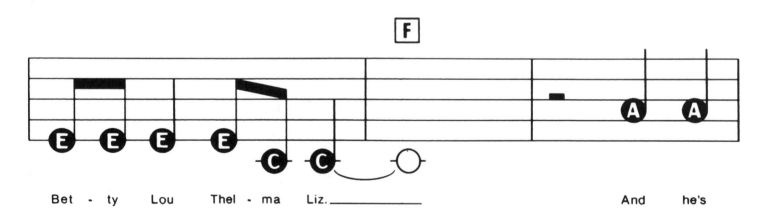

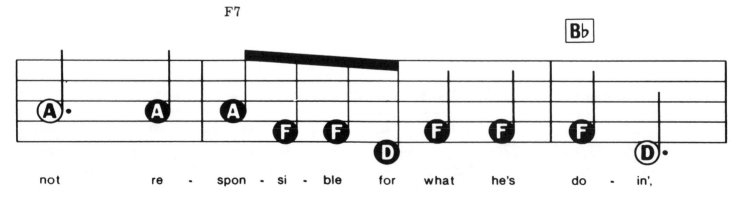

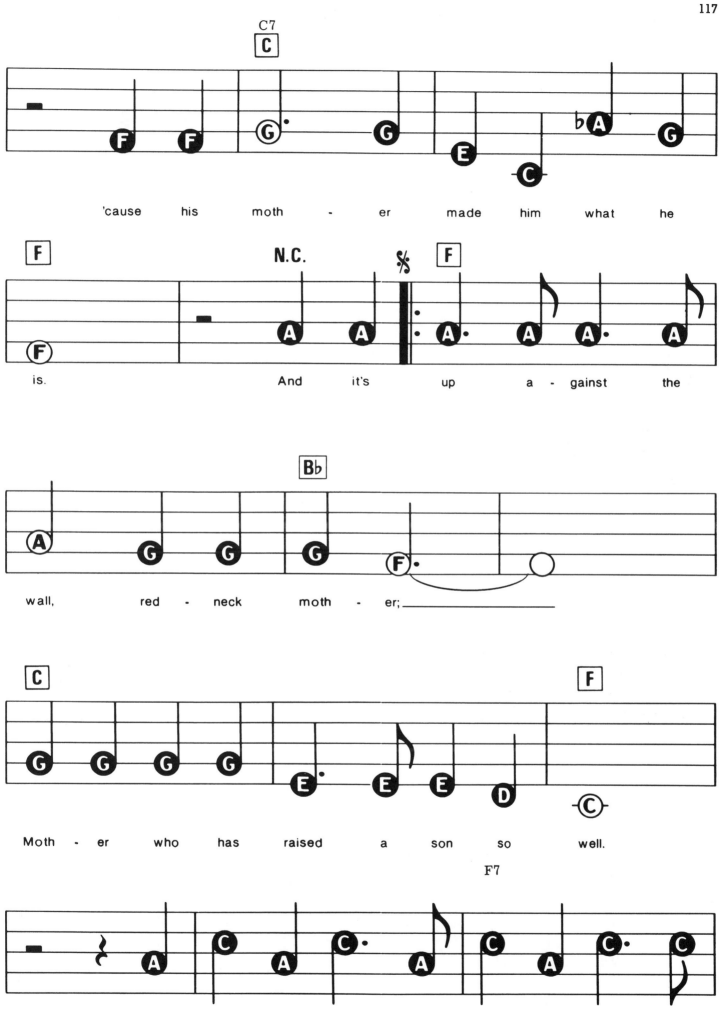

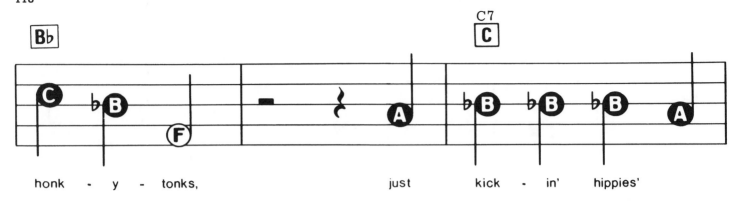

honk - y - tonks,   just   kick - in'   hippies'

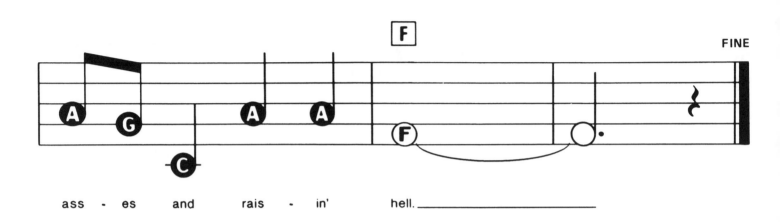

ass - es   and   rais - in'   hell. _____

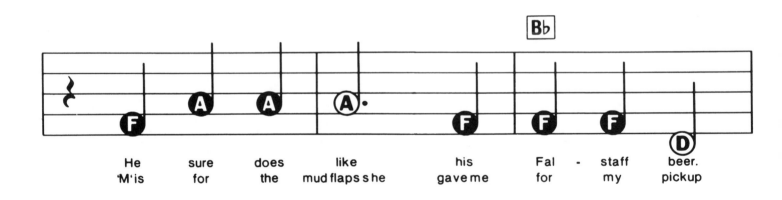

He   sure   does   like   his   Fal - staff   beer.
'M'is   for   the   mud flaps s he   gave me   for   my   pickup

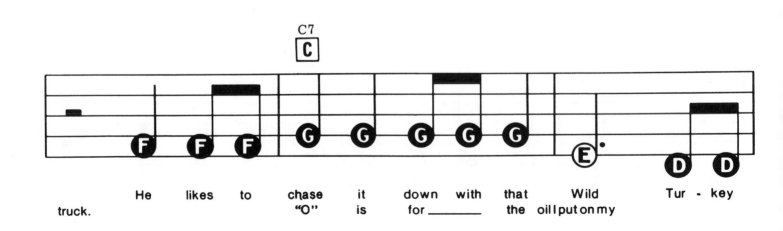

truck.   He   likes   to   chase   it   down   with   that   Wild   Tur - key
          "O"   is   for _____   the   oil I put on my

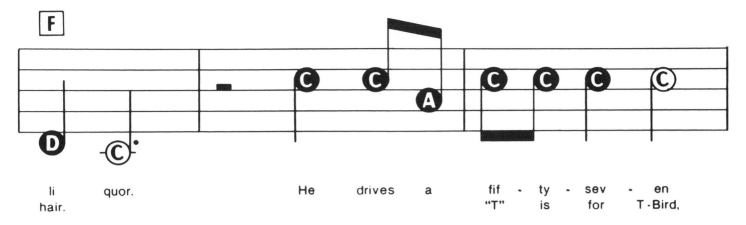

li quor. He drives a fif - ty - sev - en
hair. "T" is for T-Bird,

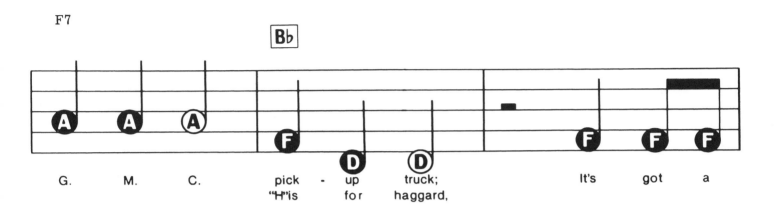

G. M. C. pick - up truck; It's got a
"H" is for haggard,

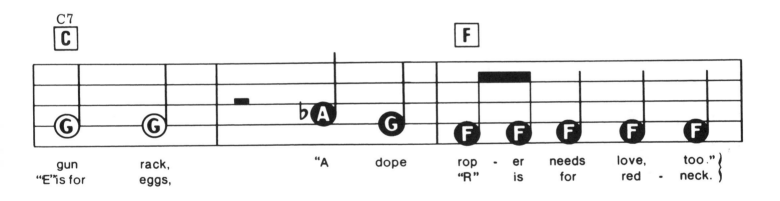

gun rack, "A dope rop - er needs love, too."
"E" is for eggs, "R" is for red - neck.

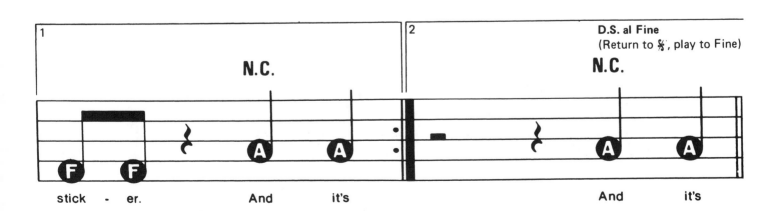

1

N.C.

stick - er. And it's

2

D.S. al Fine
(Return to 𝄋, play to Fine)

N.C.

And it's

Why Me?
(Why Me, Lord?)

Registration 2
Rhythm: Country or Swing

Words and Music by
Kris Kristofferson

You Got It

Registration 4
Rhythm: Rock or 8 Beat

Words and Music by Roy Orbison,
Jeff Lynne and Tom Petty

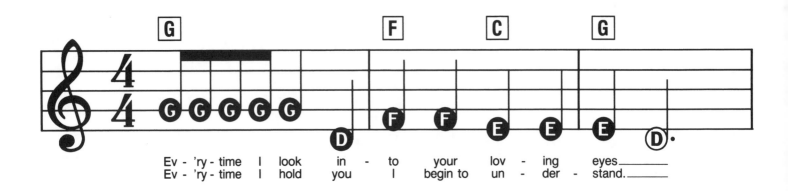

Ev - 'ry - time I look in - to your lov - ing eyes_____
Ev - 'ry - time I hold you I begin to un - der - stand._____

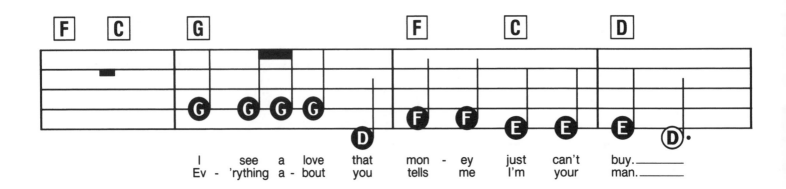

I see a love that mon - ey just can't buy._____
Ev - 'rything a - bout you tells me I'm your man._____

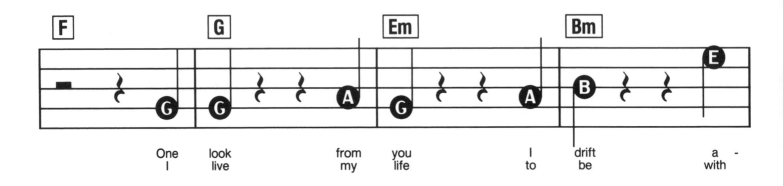

One look I live from my you life I to drift be a with

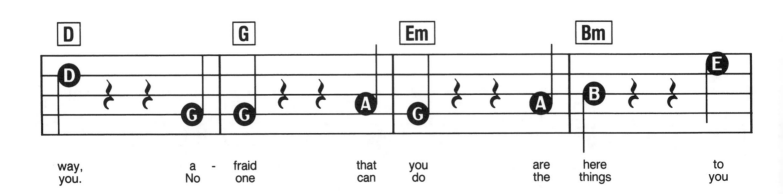

way, a - fraid that you are here to
you. No one can do the things to you

123

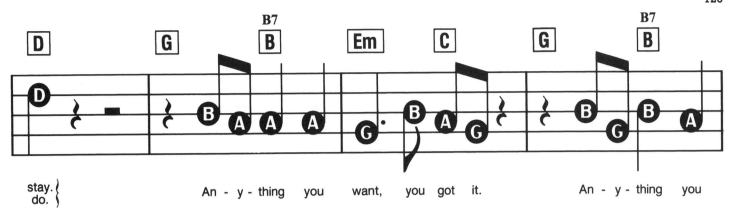

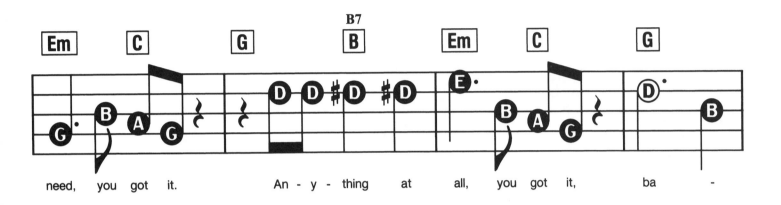

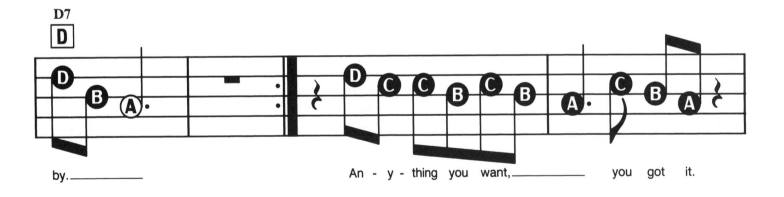

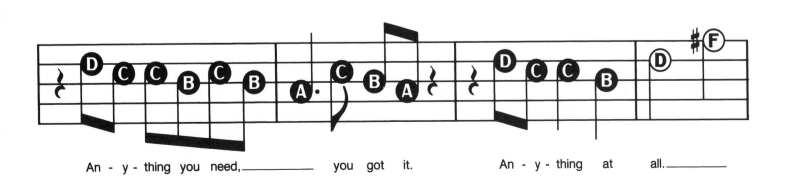

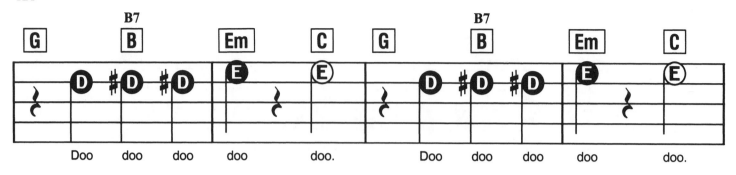

Doo doo doo doo doo. Doo doo doo doo doo.

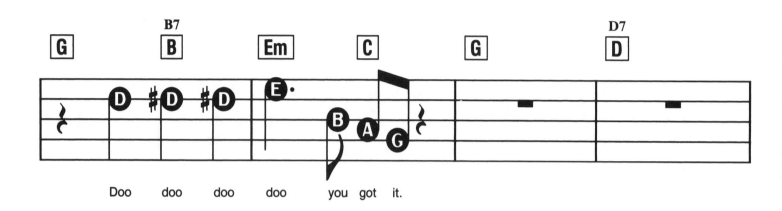

Doo doo doo doo you got it.

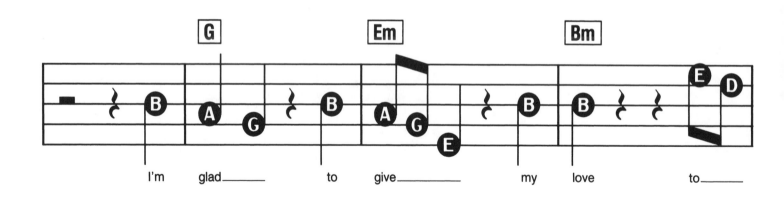

I'm glad_____ to give_____ my love to_____

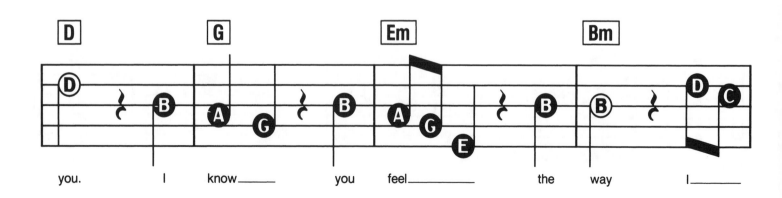

you. I know_____ you feel_____ the way I_____

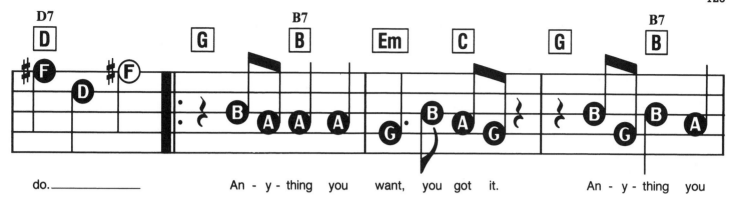

do._____ An - y - thing you want, you got it. An - y - thing you

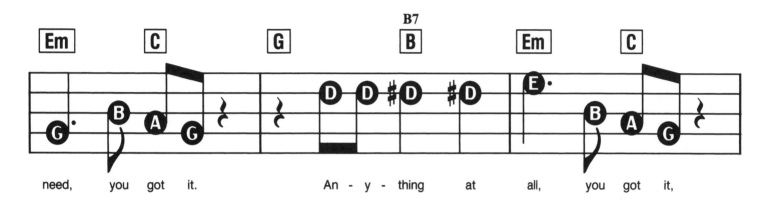

need, you got it. An - y - thing at all, you got it,

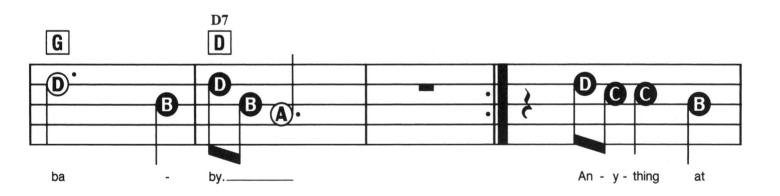

ba - by._____ An - y - thing at

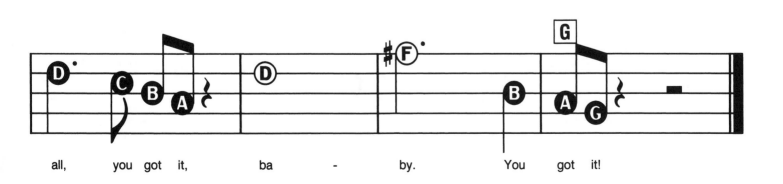

all, you got it, ba - by. You got it!

You Decorated My Life

Registration 1
Rhythm: Ballad or Fox Trot

Words and Music by Debbie Hupp
and Bob Morrison

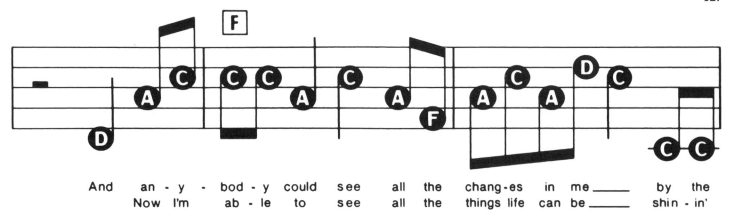

And an-y-bod-y could see all the chang-es in me ___ by the
Now I'm ab-le to see all the things life can be ___ shin-in'

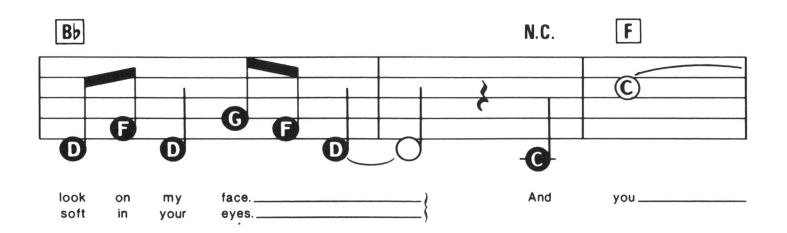

look on my face. ___ And you ___
soft in your eyes. ___

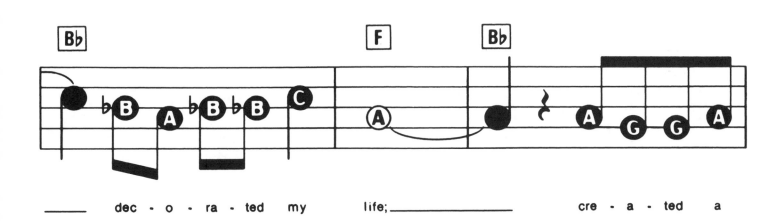

___ dec-o-ra-ted my life; ___ cre-a-ted a

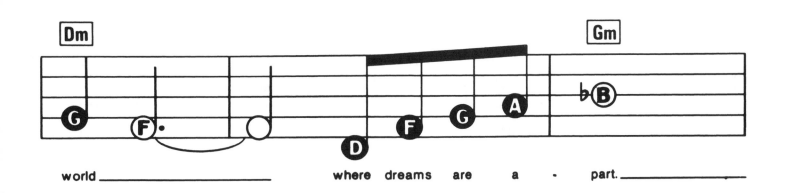

world ___ where dreams are a - part. ___

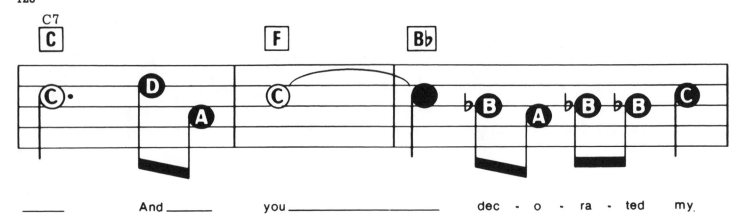

And _____ you _____ dec - o - ra - ted my.

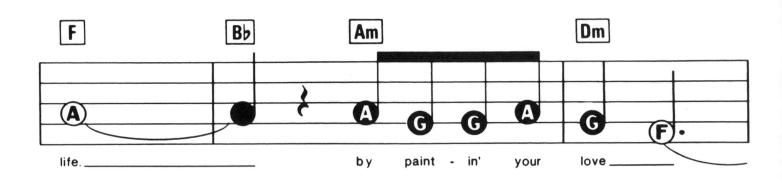

life. _____ by paint - in' your love _____

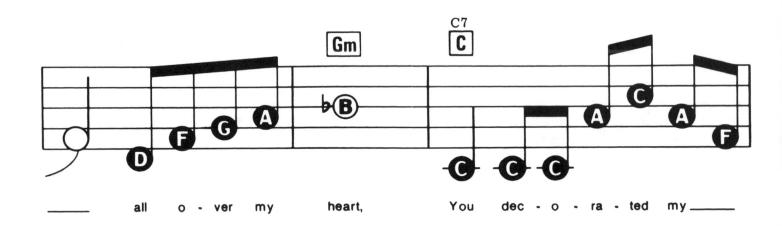

_____ all o - ver my heart, You dec - o - ra - ted my_____

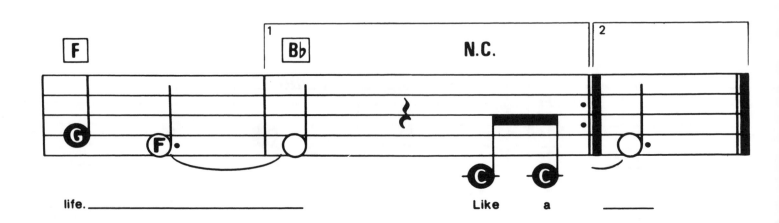

life. _____ Like a _____